Countdown to Christmas

A Family Friendly Guide to Discovering Christ's Family Tree

Written by: Andrea Dougherty and Jacquelyn Beaudry

Copyright © 2023 by Andrea Dougherty and Jacquelyn Beaudry (Blessed Little Boutique)

All rights reserved.

No portion of this book may be reproduced in any form without written permission from the publisher or author, except as permitted by U.S. copyright law. For permission requests, contact: blessedlittleboutique@gmail.com

ISBN 979-8-218-27571-6 (paperback print)

Daily Overview

Day 1	**The Stump of Jesse** *Isaiah 11:* The Story of Jesse, the Father of David	Stump
Day 2	**The Creation Story** *Genesis 1-2:* God Creates the Earth and All Living Things	Earth
Day 3	**The First Sin** *Genesis 2-3:* The Fall of Adam and Eve	Fruit
Day 4	**Noah and the Flood** *Genesis 6-9:* God's Covenant with Noah	Ark
Day 5	**The Descendants of Abraham** *Genesis 12 & 15:* God's Covenant with Abram	Stars
Day 6	**Testing Abraham** *Genesis 22:* Offering Isaac as a Sacrifice	Ram
Day 7	**Jacob's Dream** *Genesis 28:* A Ladder Reaching to Heaven From Earth	Ladder
Day 8	**Joseph and God's Providence** *Genesis 37 & 45:* A Story of Jealousy and Reconciliation	Coat
Day 9	**The Israelites** *Exodus 11-13:* Passover	Lamb
Day 10	**Moses Delivers the Israelites out of Egypt** *Exodus 14:* Parting of the Red Sea	Water
Day 11	**God Gives the People the Law** *Exodus 20:* Moses and the Ten Commandments	Tablet
Day 12	**Joshua and the Fall of Jericho** *Joshua 6, Joshua 23-24:* Joshua's Obedience and Faithfulness to God	Horn
Day 13	**Gideon** *Judges 6-8:* A Small Army and an Unlikely Victory	Soldier
Day 14	**Naomi and Ruth** *Ruth 1-4:* Ruth's Faithfulness	Grain
Day 15	**Samuel** *1 Samuel 3, 1 Samuel 10-12:* Beginning of the Kingdom of Israel	Lamp

Day 16	**David** 1 Samuel 16-17: The Brave and Faithful Shepherd	Slingshot
Day 17	**Solomon** 1 Kings 3: Prayer for a Listening Heart and the Discernment to Judge Good and Evil	Scale
Day 18	**Elijah** 1 Kings 17-18, 2 Kings 2: Elijah Fights False Gods	Fire
Day 19	**Jeremiah** Jeremiah 7, 26, 28, 29, 31: Jeremiah the Prophet and His Message of Hope	Teardrops
Day 20	**Jonah** Jonah 1-4: Jonah and the Whale	Whale
Day 21	**John** Luke 3, John 1, Matthew 11: John the Baptist Proclaims the Coming of the Messiah	Shell
Day 22	**Mary** Matthew 1, Luke 1: Mary, the Mother of Jesus	Mary
Day 23	**Elizabeth** Luke 1: Mary Visits her Cousin Elizabeth, the Mother of John the Baptist	Elizabeth and Mary
Day 24	**Joseph** Matthew 1, Luke 2: Mary's Husband and Jesus' Earthly Father	Toolbox
Day 25	**Jesus** Luke 2, Matthew 2: The Birth of Our Lord	Nativity

The Tradition of the Jesse Tree

The Jesse Tree is a tradition rooted in Christianity that traces its origins back to the medieval period. It is a way of visualizing Christ's family members who came long before him by using a tree or a branch to symbolize the family tree of Jesse, the father of King David. The name "Jesse Tree" is taken from a passage in the Bible's book of Isaiah that refers to the coming of a Messiah from the family tree of Jesse. You will dive deeply into that Bible passage on Day 1.

During the four weeks of Advent, which is the period leading up to Christmas, families sometimes create or display a small Jesse Tree. Each day, a new ornament or symbol representing a different person or event from the Old Testament is added to the tree. These symbols often include figures like Adam and Eve, Noah, Abraham, Moses, and others, as well as significant events like the parting of the Red Sea and the giving of the Ten Commandments. The progression of symbols helps tell the story of salvation history leading up to the birth of our Savior, Jesus Christ.

The Jesse Tree tradition serves as a way to reflect on the importance of Jesus' birth in the context of the broader biblical narrative. It is a visual reminder of how Jesus' lineage and birth are intertwined with the history of God's relationship with humanity as told in the Old Testament stories.

This book was written to be a simple guide for families of all ages. There are 25 stories that correspond with 25 ornaments, each representing the 25 days in December leading up to Christmas. Some of the stories are simple for young learners, and some are quite complex. Repeated, yearly exposure will help your whole family understand the journey of God's chosen people and will, hopefully, be a guide during your own journey in life. You may use your family Christmas tree to hang the ornaments, or hang them on a smaller, separate tree.

Advent Family Prayers

Lord Jesus,

Master of both the light and the darkness,

send your Holy Spirit upon our preparations for Christmas.

We who have so much to do

seek quiet spaces to hear your voice each day.

We who are anxious over many things

look forward to your coming among us.

We who are blessed in so many ways long for

the complete joy of your kingdom.

We whose hearts are heavy

seek the joy of your presence.

We are your people,

walking in darkness, yet seeking the light.

To you we say, "Come Lord Jesus!"

Amen.

- Henri J.M. Nouwen

God of Love,

Your son, Jesus, is your greatest gift to us.

He is a sign of your love.

Help us walk in that love during the weeks of Advent,

As we wait and prepare for His coming.

We pray in the name of Jesus, our Savior.

Amen.

-Author Unknown

Day 1

The Stump of Jesse: The Story of Jesse, the Father of David
Isaiah 11

Can you name some of the people in your immediate and extended family? How are you related? Did you know that Jesus has a family tree, too? It is filled with important people who lived long before His birth on Christmas day. The stories of Jesus' family members are told in the Old Testament of the Bible. These stories help us understand God's promises and prepare us for the coming of Jesus in the New Testament.

In the Bible, the book of Isaiah says, "But a shoot shall sprout from the stump of Jesse, and from his roots a bud shall blossom." (Isaiah 11:1). Jesse is one of Jesus' relatives and the father of King David. Do not worry, you will learn more about him later. Now, look at the stump. It symbolizes sin and life without Jesus. The blossom represents forgiveness, hope, and a new life with our Savior, Jesus.

Activities:
1. Take out the Bible and examine the difference between the Old and New Testament.
2. Discuss your family tree. How does it grow and change like a real tree? Create a simple tree for your family and study the artwork of Jesus' family tree.
3. Find the ornament with the stump and hang it on your family Jesse Tree.

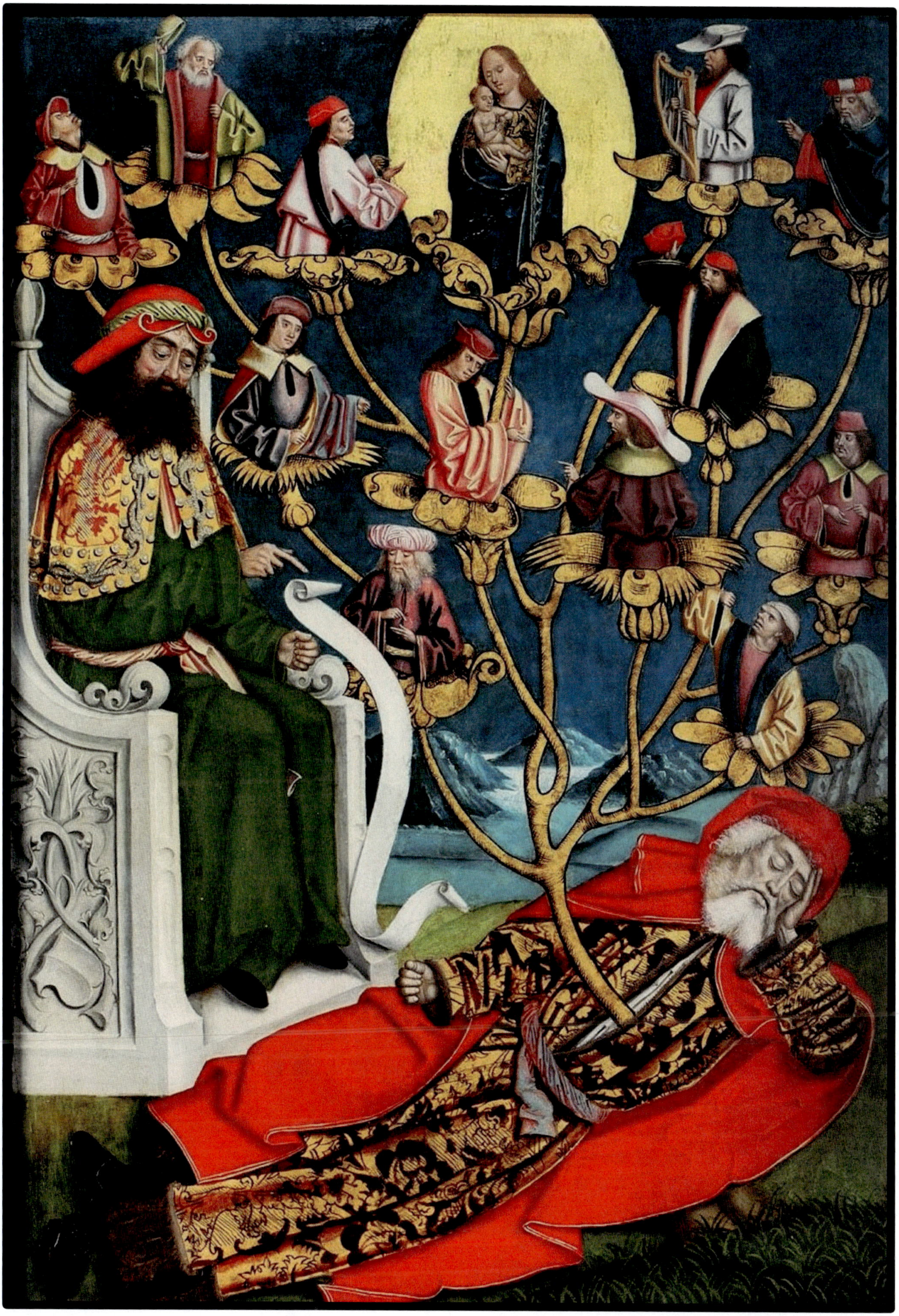

Day 2

The Creation Story: God Creates the Earth and All Living Things
Genesis 1-2

In Genesis chapters 1 and 2, the Bible tells us that God created day and night on the first day. On the second day, He created the sky. On the third day, He created the Earth, sea, plants, and trees. On the fourth day, He created the sun, moon, and stars. On the fifth day, God created birds and sea creatures. On the sixth day, God created man and land animals. On the seventh day, God rested and admired the goodness of His work. He blessed the seventh day and made it holy. What is something that God created that you are thankful for?

Did you notice that God has not created woman yet? After God created all the animals, He knew that none of them were good partners for the man. It is not good for the man to be alone. God created woman to be a partner for the man. The names of the first man and woman are Adam and Eve. Not only are they the very first people ever created, they are also the first people on Christ's family tree. Because of Adam and Eve, we are all a part of the same family.... mankind.

Activities:
1. Say a prayer of thanksgiving as a family for the creations you are most thankful.
2. Go on a family walk and appreciate the beauty in all that God has created.
3. Look closely at the picture. Can you spot Adam and Eve?
4. Find the Earth ornament and hang it on your family Jesse Tree.

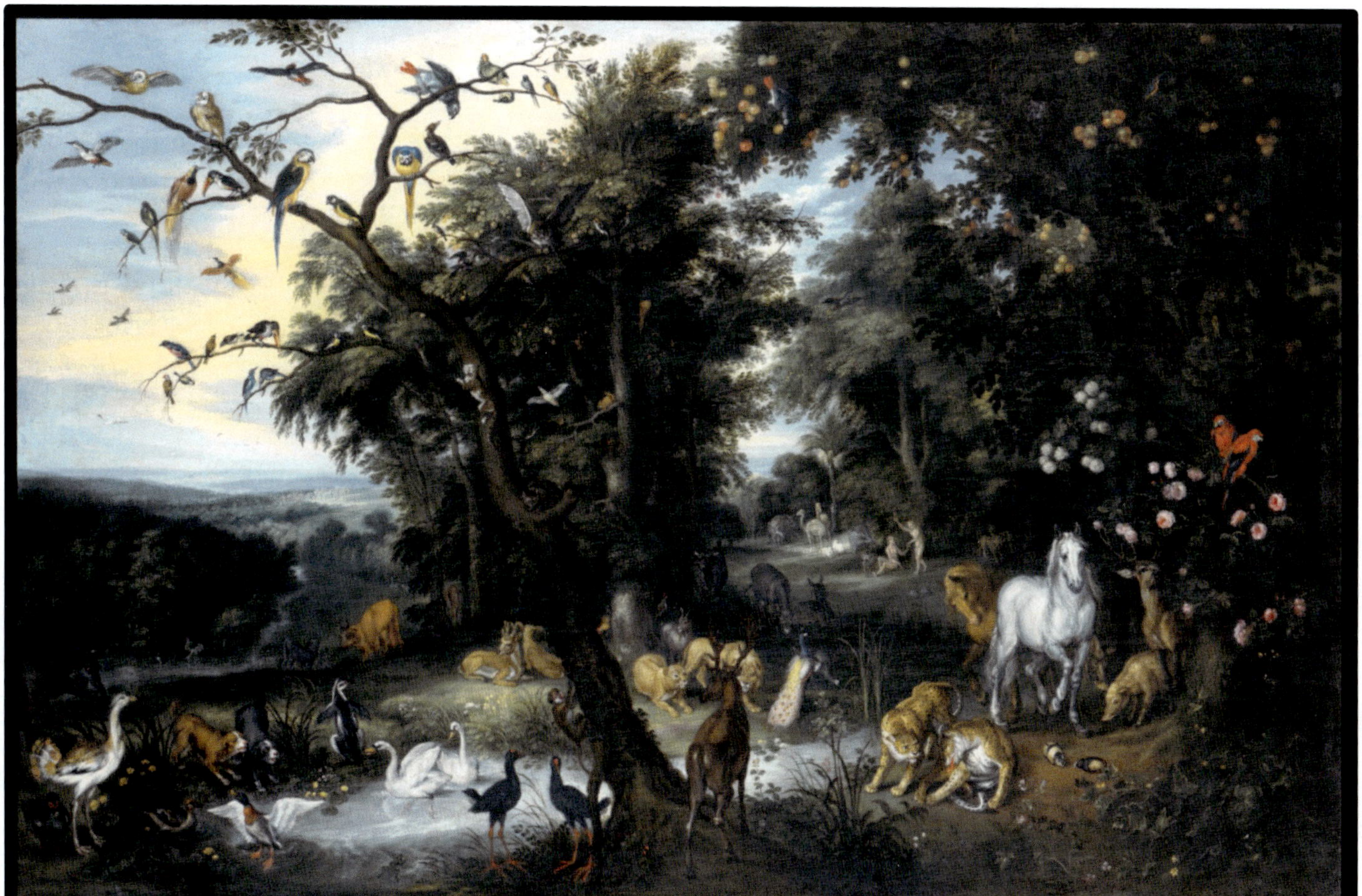

Day 3

The First Sin: The Fall of Adam and Eve
Genesis 2-3

In Genesis chapters 2 and 3, God creates a beautiful garden in Eden. In the middle of the garden, God places the Tree of Knowledge of Good and Bad. He places Adam in the garden to care for it and tells him that he may eat from any of the trees, except for the Tree of Knowledge. Just as God gave Adam and Eve a choice to obey or disobey, He also gives us the same choice. God is our loving Father, and He wants what is good for us. Can you think of a time when you obeyed and a time when you disobeyed? How did it make you feel?

When Eve is created, she joins Adam in the Garden of Eden. A cunning snake appears to Eve and tricks her into disobeying God, eating fruit from the Tree of Knowledge and even sharing the fruit with Adam. The snake was sneaky and made Eve question what God had commanded. She was tempted by the beauty of the fruit and did not see how it could be bad when it looked so good. Adam and Eve ate the fruit. This was the first sin because they disobeyed God. We must always trust that God has a plan for us and knows what is best for us, even if it is not what we want or think is best for ourselves. God was disappointed in Adam and Eve. He gave them serious consequences that would affect all mankind.

Activities:
1. Think about a time when you obeyed. Thank God for guiding you to make the right choice.
2. Think about a time when you disobeyed. Ask God to forgive you of your sin and to help you learn to trust Him.
3. Find the fruit ornament and hang it on your family Jesse Tree.

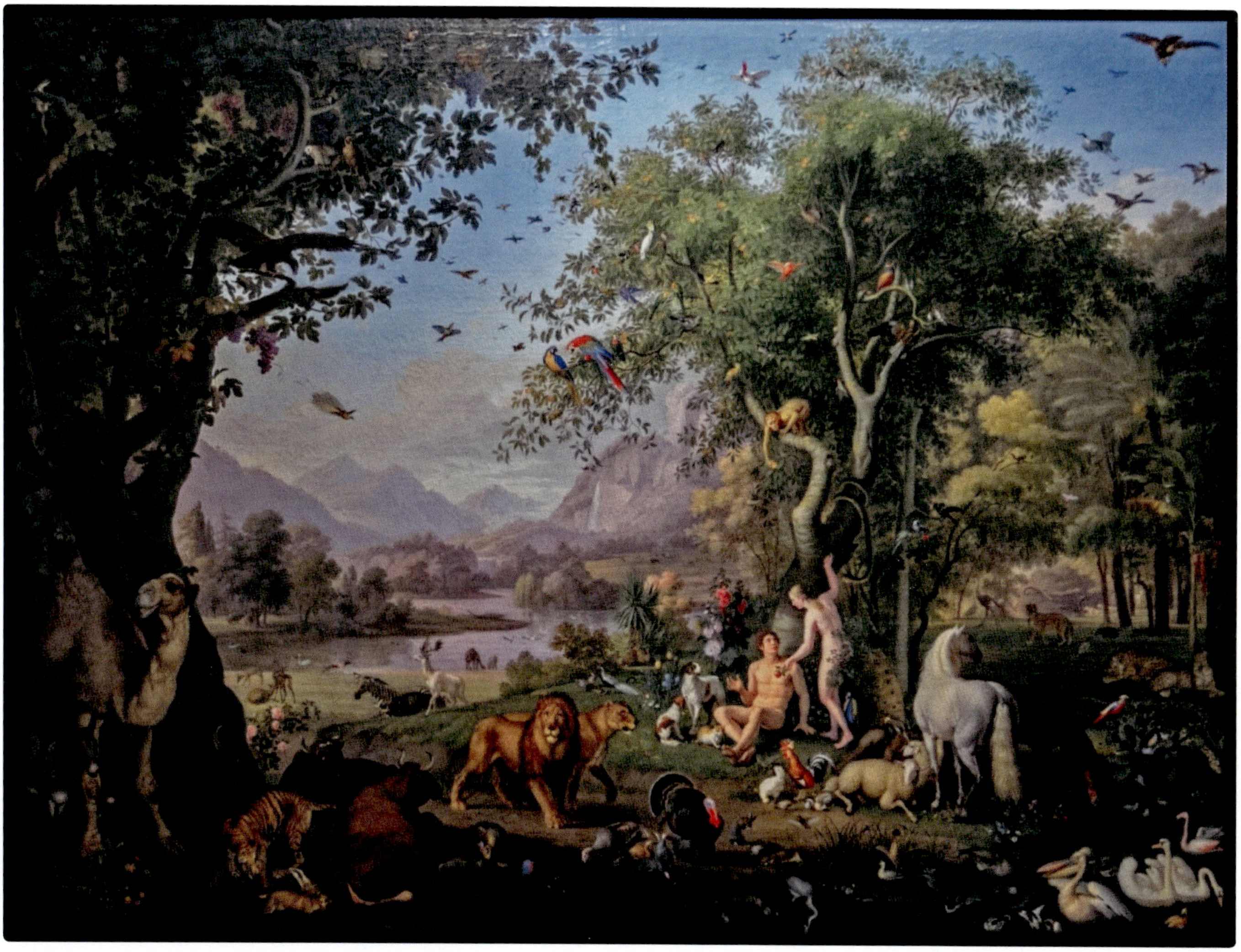

Day 4

Noah and the Flood: God's Covenant with Noah
Genesis 6-9

Yesterday, you learned about the first sin. Do you remember what a sin is? Well, unfortunately, Adam and Eve's descendants continue to sin and disobey God. The Bible tells us that God planned a great flood to destroy the Earth, which would cause all living things to die.

Noah is a descendant of Adam and Eve. God was pleased with Noah and saw that he was a good man who obeyed and loved God with all his heart. Because of this, God chose Noah to save the human family.

God commands Noah to build an ark to save his family from the flood. He was instructed to bring his family and a pair of every living creature, one male and one female, onto the ark. Close your eyes and imagine how enormous the ark must have been in order to hold every type of animal on Earth. Noah obeyed and did all that God commanded. Genesis 7:23 says, "The LORD wiped out every living thing on earth: man and cattle, the creeping things and the birds of the air; all were wiped out from the earth. Only Noah and those with him in the ark were left."

After the flood, God set a rainbow in the clouds to serve as a symbol of his covenant (which is a promise) with the Earth that He would never again use a flood to destroy humanity.

Activities:
1. Draw a picture to go along with the story of Noah's Ark. Do not forget to include a rainbow.
2. Find the ornament with the ark and hang it on your family Jesse Tree.

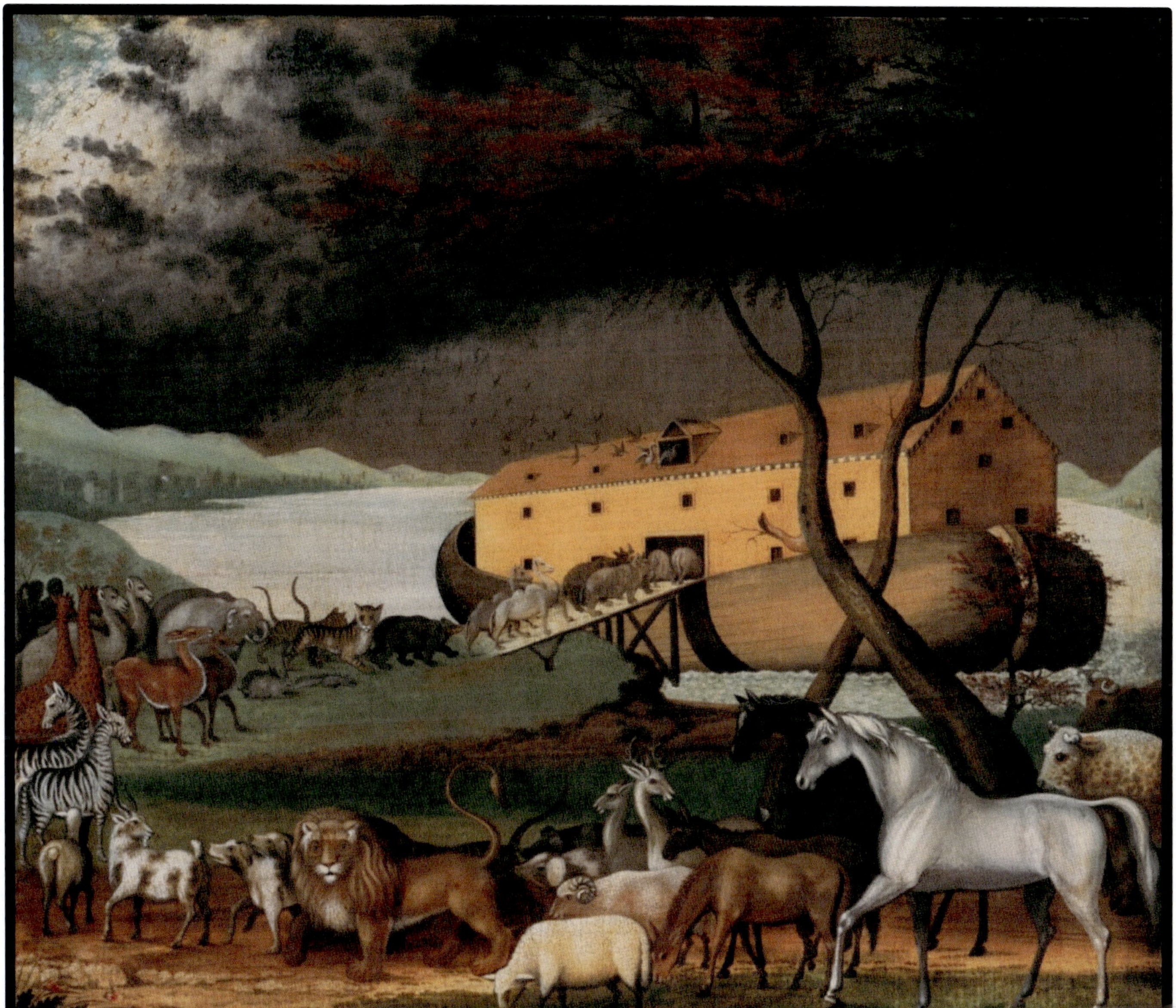

Day 5

The Descendants of Abraham: God's Covenant with Abram
Genesis 12 & 15

Have you ever tried to count all the stars in the sky?

In Genesis chapters 12 and 15, we learn about Abram and how he put his faith and trust in God. Abram was a good man, and he had a wife named Sarai. Together, they owned many sheep and cattle, but they did not have any children.

One day, God appeared to Abram and told him to pack up all his things and to move to the land of Canaan with his wife. God said that He would bless Abram and his wife, and that his family would be great. Abram trusted God and did as He had asked. He and his wife packed up their belongings and moved far away to Canaan.

Then, one night, God appeared to Abram again. Abram talked to God and said he was sad that he did not have any children. God told Abram to look up at the stars in the sky. He said that one day Abram and Sarai would have a son, and that son would go on to have children, and those children would go on to have more children, and eventually, there would be as many as the stars in the sky. Abram did ask God how this would happen, but God made a promise to Abram and said that because of Abram and his strong faith, all people on Earth would be blessed, and God always keeps His promises.

Activities:
1. Take out a piece of paper and try to draw as many stars as possible.
2. Find the ornament with stars and hang it on your family Jesse Tree.
3. Tomorrow is the Feast of Saint Nicholas. Adults- Discuss St. Nicholas' life with your children. Fill their shoes with goodies to be discovered tomorrow morning.

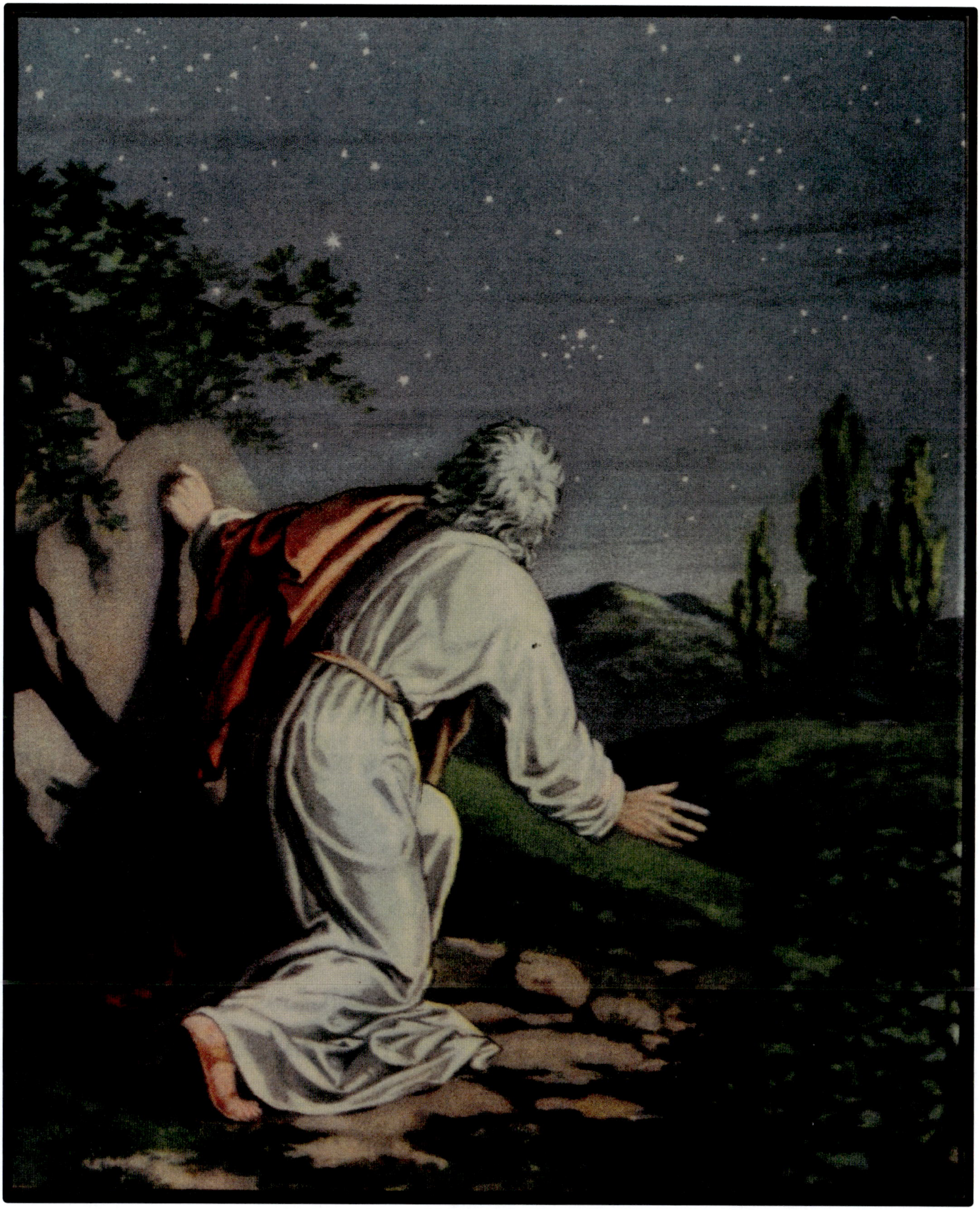

Day 6

Testing Abraham: Offering Isaac as a Sacrifice
Genesis 22

Remember yesterday, how we learned about Abram and how he trusted God? Later, Abram's name changed to Abraham and Sarai to Sarah, and today we learn about another time Abraham had complete faith and trust in God. Think about a time when you were scared or nervous about something. Did you say a pray and have faith and trust in God? How about in the people you love the most?

After Abraham and Sarah had moved to Canaan as God had asked, God did as He promised, and Abraham and his wife, Sarah, had a baby boy named Isaac. They loved Isaac so much and took good care of him.

One day, God asked Abraham to sacrifice his only son, Isaac. God was testing Abraham's faith in Him. Abraham and Sarah thought and prayed about this very hard, and although it made them sad, they trusted that God had a plan. So, Abraham took his son Isaac to the place where God had asked. Before Abraham could go further with God's instructions, an angel appeared to Abraham and told him to stop what he was doing. He said that God saw how much Abraham and Isaac believed in God and God's plan. Abraham saw a ram nearby and grabbed it by its horns to offer as a sacrifice in place of his son.

Because Abraham and Isaac did what God had asked, God said He would bless Abraham and his family in many ways. This story really teaches us to believe in God and trust His plan, even when things are scary.

Activities:
1. Think about the people in your life that are most important to you. Say a prayer thanking God for them.
2. Find the ornament with a ram and hang it on your family Jesse Tree.

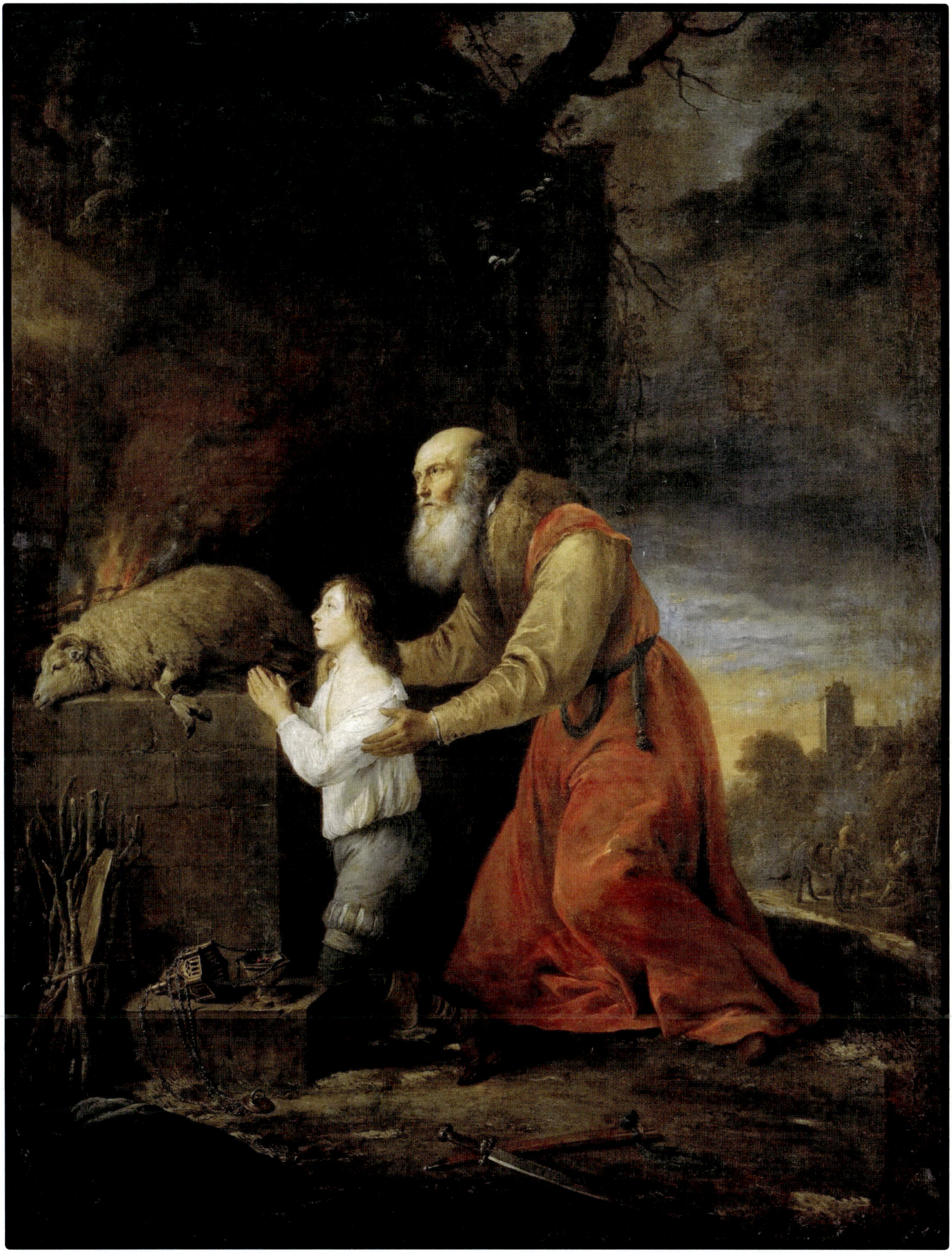

Day 7

Jacob's Dream: A Ladder Reaching to Heaven From Earth
Genesis 28

Do you dream at night when you sleep? Do you remember a dream you have had recently? Today, we will learn about Jacob and an important dream he had. Jacob is the son of Isaac and Rebecca. Remember Isaac from our story yesterday? Isaac is the son of Abraham and Sarah.

One day, Jacob set out on a journey to the city of Haran. It was a long journey, so he would stop in different places to sleep overnight. One night, he grabbed a stone to rest his head on when he stopped to sleep. How uncomfortable! When he fell asleep, he began having a dream. In the dream, there was a ladder that rested on the ground and reached up to Heaven. Angels went up and down the ladder, and God stood beside him. God told Jacob that He would give Jacob and his descendants the land he was sitting on and bless him. God said that He would protect Jacob and stay with him always.

When Jacob woke up, he cried out, "How awesome is this shrine! This is nothing else but an abode of God, and that is the gateway to heaven!" (Genesis 28:17). Jacob took the stone he was lying on, and he placed it there as a memorial, and he poured oil on it. He named this new place Bethel, which means "House of God."

This is a fantastic story of how God blessed Jacob, but it also shows how God is giving us a way to get to Heaven one day.

Activities:
1. Make a paper chain counting down the days until Christmas. Think of the chain leading to Christmas, like the ladder that led to Heaven.
2. Find the ornament with a ladder and hang it on your family Jesse Tree.

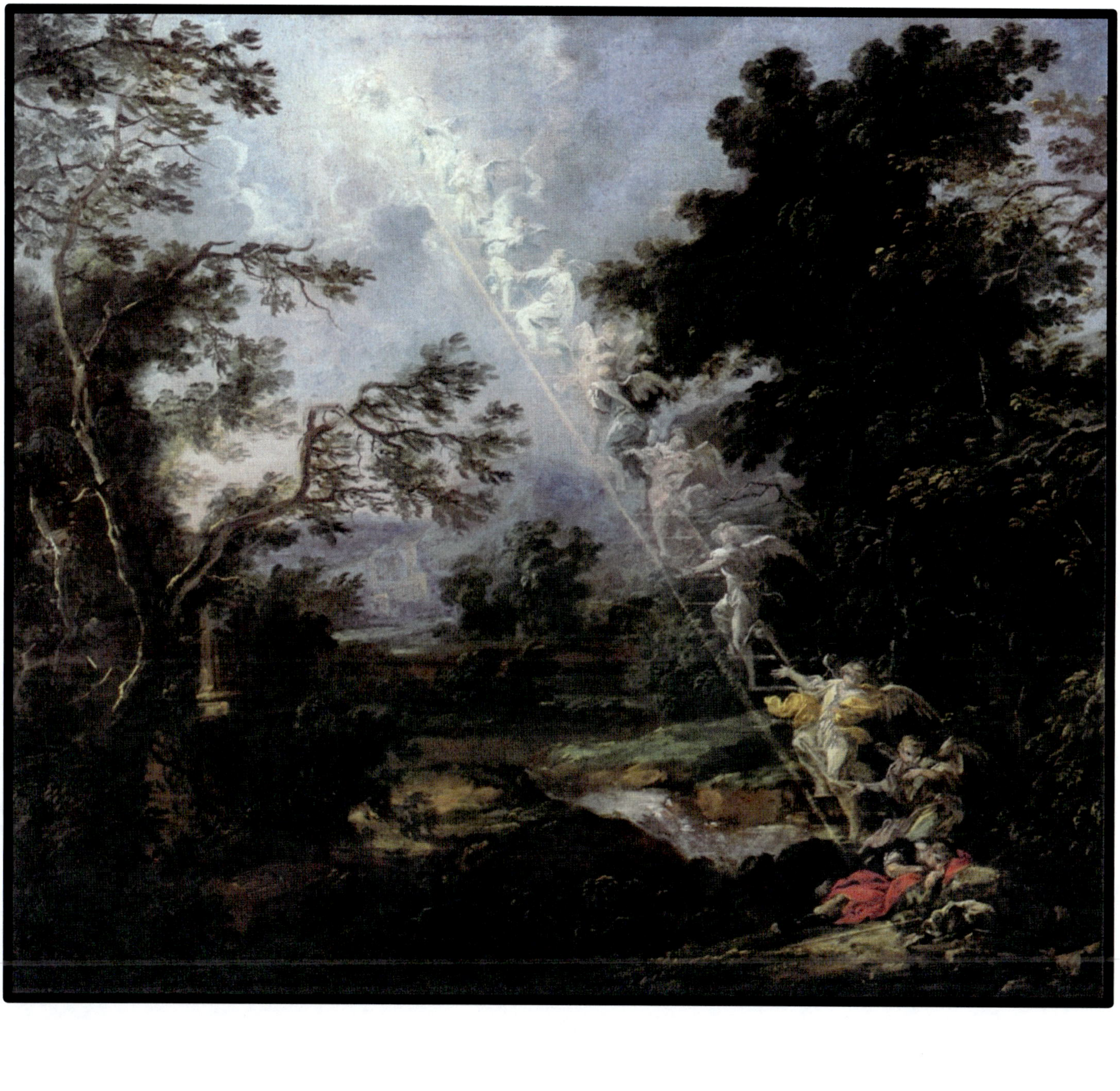

Day 8

Joseph and God's Providence: A Story of Jealousy and Reconciliation
Genesis 37 & 45

Yesterday, we talked about Jacob and his special dream. Well, today, we will read about Jacob's son, Joseph. Keep in mind that God changed Jacob's name to Israel. Israel gave Joseph a long tunic (like a robe or a long coat), which made his brothers very jealous and angry.

One day, when Joseph and his brothers were working in the fields, Joseph started telling his brothers about a dream that he had where things were bowing down to him. This made his brothers even more angry. Joseph continued having similar dreams where his parents and brothers bowed down to him. The brothers were getting angrier and angrier with Joseph's dreams and finally had had enough.

The brothers came up with a plan to get rid of Joseph. So, they took him to an empty cave and left him there without any food or water. Later, they decided to sell Joseph to the Egyptians so they could make money. They took Joseph's coat, and dipped it in goat's blood, and brought it to their father, Israel. Israel believed his son, Joseph, was dead, and he was so sad.

In the meantime, God raised Joseph to a high position in the Pharaoh's court. Later, Israel sent his sons to the court of Egypt to buy food. They stood before their brother, Joseph, and did not even recognize him. They bowed down before him, just as Joseph had predicted. Eventually, they realized it was their brother, and they wept joyfully. In the end, Joseph saved Israel and all his family from the deadly famine by moving them to Egypt.

Activities:
1. Share with your family what you learned from the story of Joseph.
2. Have you ever felt jealous? Share what this felt like with your family.
3. Find the ornament with a coat and hang it on your family Jesse Tree.

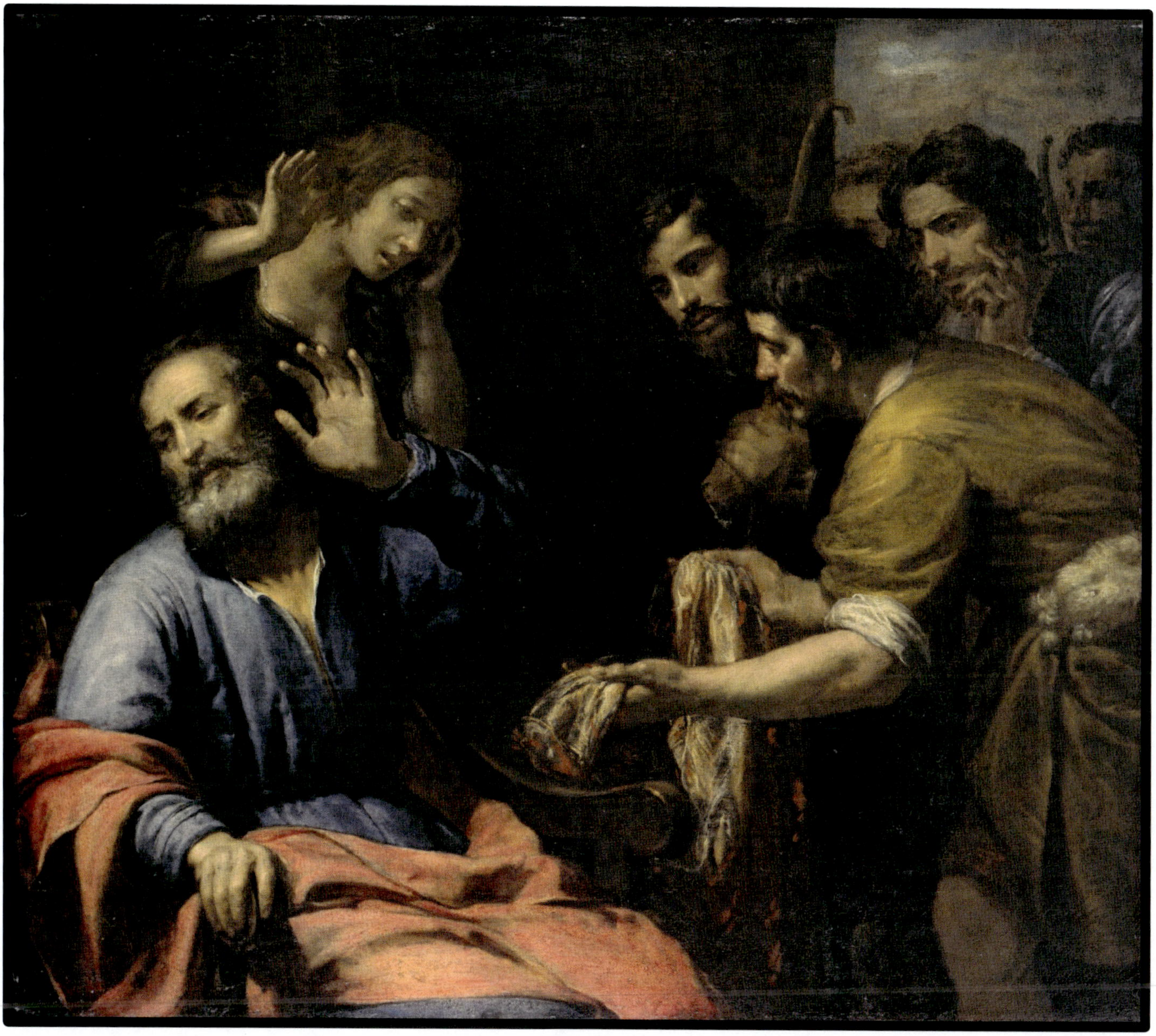

Day 9

The Israelites: Passover
Exodus 11-13

Have you ever passed on a turn or sat out during an activity or event? What does the word "Passover" make you think of? Today, we will learn how God passed over His chosen people, the Israelites, and saved them from death. Let's dig a little deeper! Remember that the Israelites are living in the land of Egypt as slaves to the Egyptian people. The Egyptian Pharaoh has a hardened heart and refuses to set the Israelites free. Because the Egyptians will not free God's people, God will strike down every firstborn person or animal in the land of Egypt. God promised to save His chosen people, the Israelites. God uses His faithful follower, Moses, to share God's plan with the Israelites to spare their lives. For Israelites to be saved from death, they are to slaughter a lamb and spread its blood on their two doorposts and lintel. Exodus 12:23 states, "For when the LORD goes by to strike down the Egyptians, seeing the blood on the lintel and the two doorposts, the LORD will pass over that door and not let the destroyer come into your houses to strike you down." The Israelites obeyed God and were saved. That same night, the Pharaoh heard the crying of the Egyptian people and realized that he could not defeat God. The Pharaoh immediately went to Moses and told him to take his people and leave Egypt. They are FREE! God is good. He keeps His promises and protects His chosen people. Tomorrow, you will read about the long and miraculous journey the Israelites took out of Egypt with Moses as their leader.

Activities:
1. Study the artwork. Do you see the angel protecting the Israelite home? Can you find the lamb? How about the markings on the doorposts and lintel?
2. Find the ornament with the Passover lamb and hang it on your family Jesse Tree.

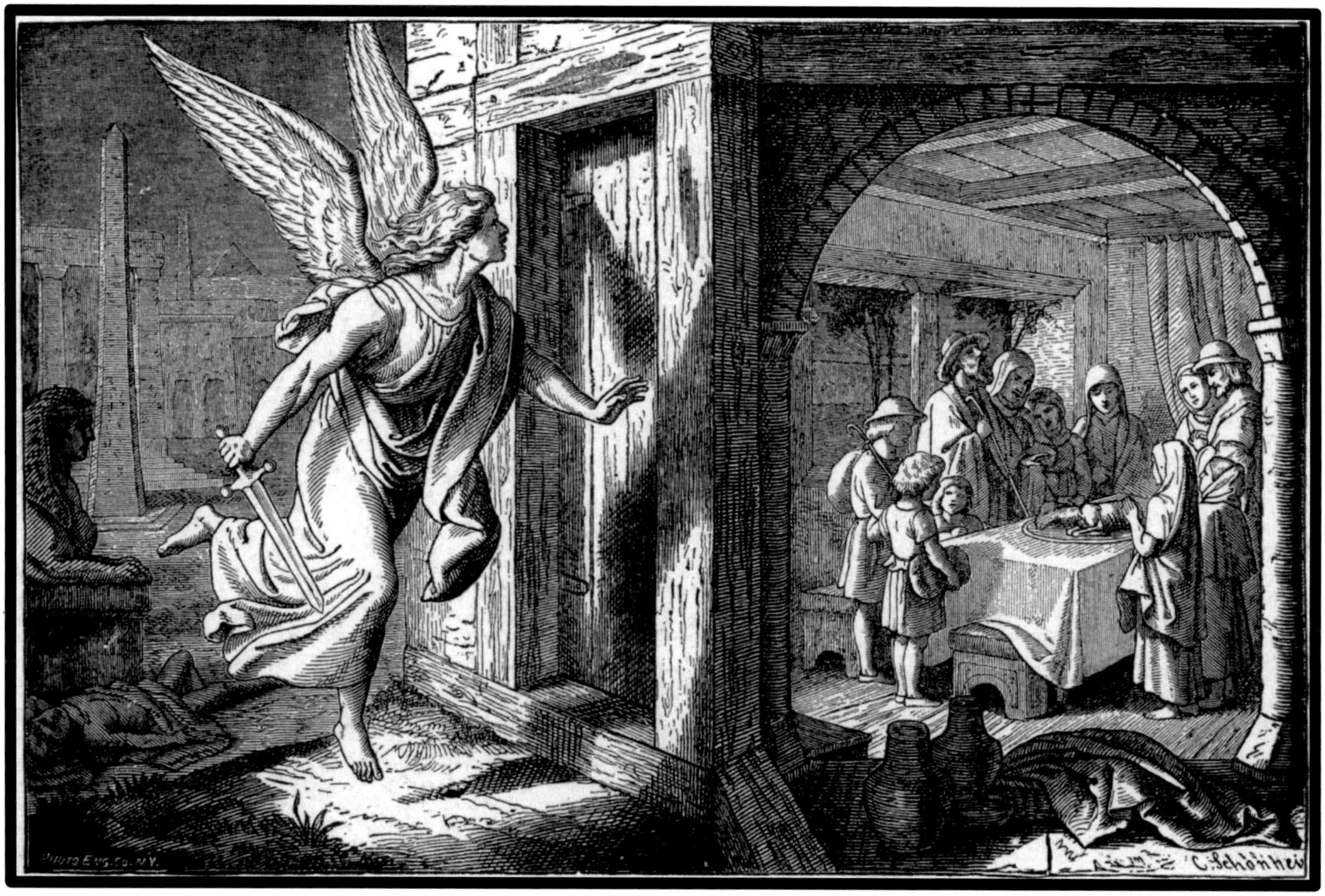

Day 10

Moses Delivers the Israelites out of Egypt: Parting of the Red Sea
Exodus 14

Remember yesterday we read about the Passover and how the Israelites were set free? Today, we are going to talk about how God chose Moses to lead the Israelites out of Egypt. Along their journey, God continued to show Moses and the Israelites the way. In the meantime, back in Egypt, Pharaoh started thinking about how he set the Israelites free and he started second-guessing himself. So, he decided to chase after them to have them come back to Egypt. Pharaoh gathered his soldiers and chariots and sent them after the Israelites. Eventually, the soldiers caught up with the Israelites near the Red Sea.

When the Israelites spotted the Egyptians, they cried out to the Lord. They were scared because there was nowhere to go, as the Red Sea was all that was in front of them and the soldiers behind them. They started questioning Moses and why he brought them into the desert if they would end up dying. They felt it would have been better to be slaves to the Egyptians than to die in the desert. Moses responded by saying, "Fear not! Stand your ground, and you will see the victory the LORD will win for you today. These Egyptians whom you see today you will never see again." (Exodus 14:13).

God told Moses to stretch out his hand and split the sea in two. So, a dark cloud moved behind the Israelites, Moses stretched out his hand, and God divided the Red Sea in two, with dry land in the middle and water like a wall on both sides. The Israelites passed through on dry land, and the Egyptians followed, but once the Israelites were through, Moses stretched out his hand again, and God put the sea back together, wiping out all Egyptian soldiers. The Israelites saw what God did for them, and they believed.

Activities:
1. Fill a shallow dish with water. Using a straw, blow air into the water to symbolize the parting of the Red Sea.
2. Find the ornament with the water and hang it on your family Jesse Tree.

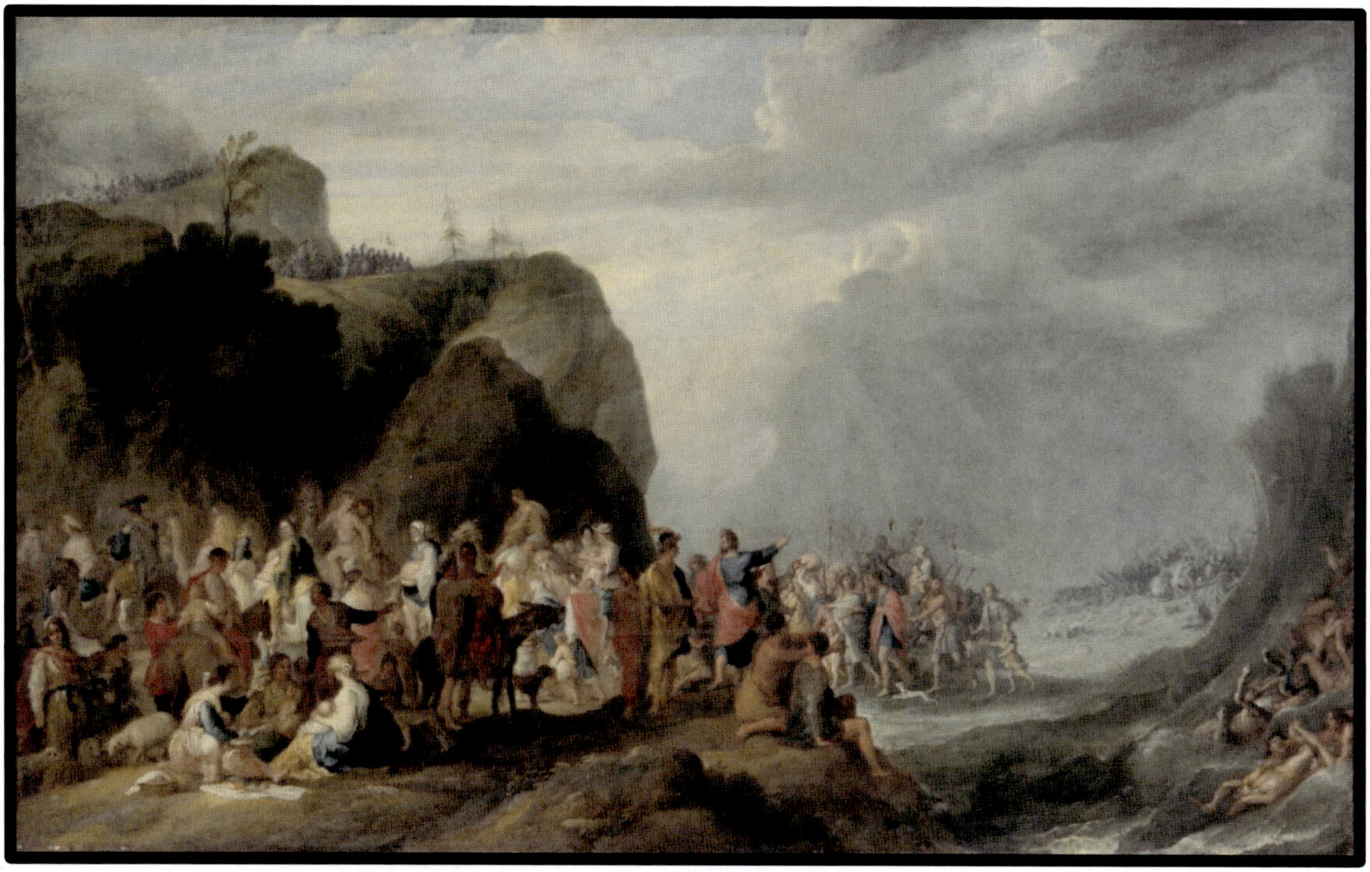

Day 11

God Gives the People the Law: Moses and the Ten Commandments
Exodus 20

Moses goes up to the mountain of God, Mount Sinai. God reminds him of what He has done for the Israelite people: "I am the LORD your God, who brought you out of the land of Egypt, out of the house of slavery." (Exodus 20:2). God gives His people rules, or instructions, to live by. We call these the Ten Commandments. God loves us so much He wants us to be set apart as His chosen people. Your loving actions and obedience to our Heavenly Father will also help set you apart.

1. I, the Lord, am your God. You shall not have other gods besides me.
2. You shall not take the name of the Lord, your God, in vain.
3. Remember to keep holy the Lord's day.
4. Honor your father and your mother.
5. You shall not kill.
6. You shall not commit adultery.
7. You shall not steal.
8. You shall not bear false witness against your neighbor.
9. You shall not covet your neighbor's wife.
10. You shall not covet your neighbor's goods.

Activities:
1. Review the Ten Commandments with your family. Which commandments are easy for you to follow, and which are hard for you to follow? When you pray, ask Jesus to help you.
2. Find the ornament with the tablet and hang it on your family Jesse Tree.

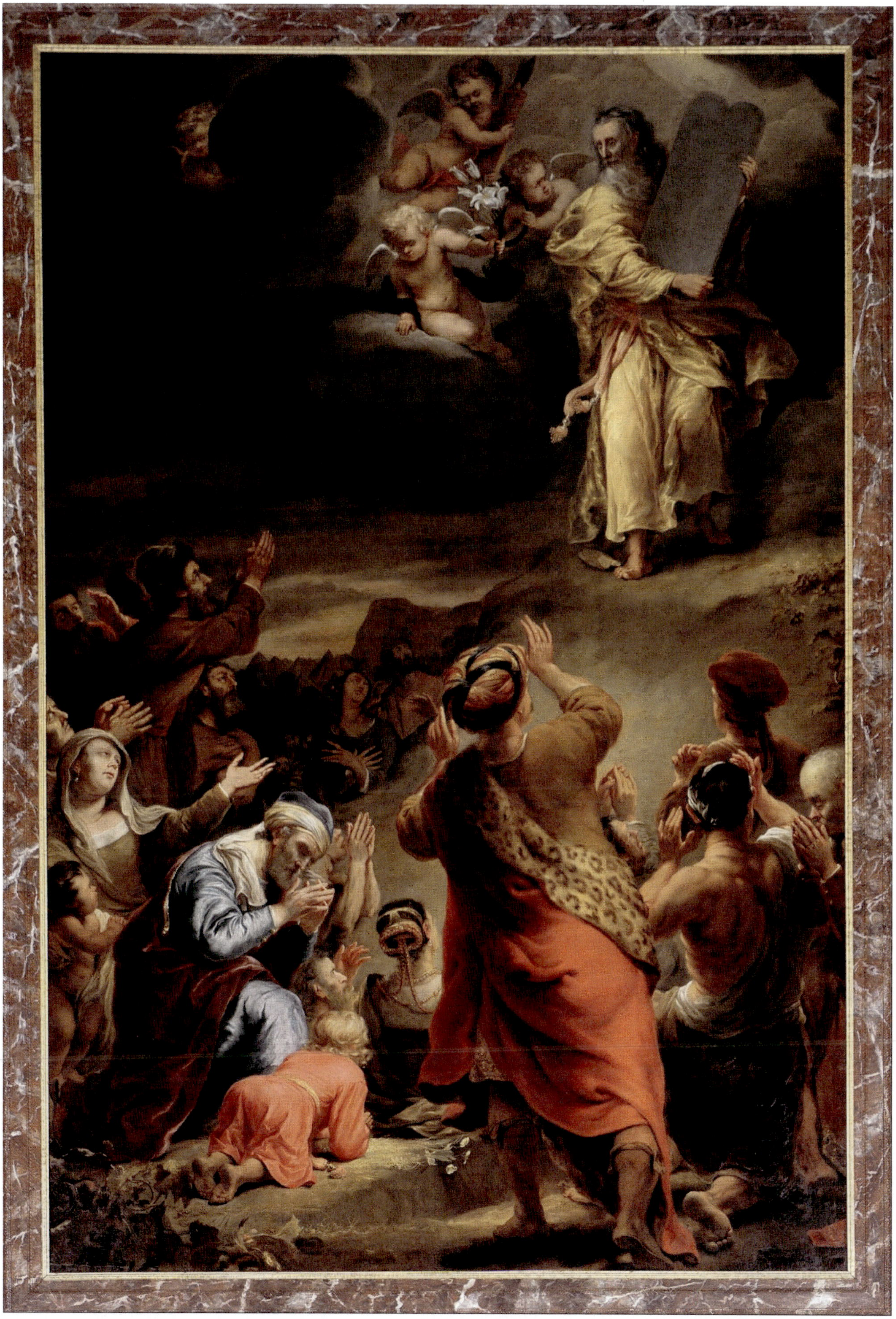

Day 12

Joshua and the Fall of Jericho: Joshua's Obedience and Faithfulness to God
Joshua 6 & 23-24

After Moses died, God chose Joshua to lead the Israelites. God tells Joshua to lead the people of Israel in an attack on the city of Jericho to take possession of the land God had promised them. God promised Joshua that He would be with him and protect him along the way, just as He had done for Moses.

Do you know how long the Israelites wandered in the desert? It was 40 years! That is a really long time! Back in the day, cities were surrounded by tall walls for protection, and Jericho was one of them. God gave Joshua detailed instructions on how to win the Battle of Jericho. First, he sent spies into the city to see what information they could find. They met a woman named Rahab, who allowed the spies in to hide. Rahab knows she has not been a woman of God, so she asks if she and her family can be saved if she helps the Israelites take over Jericho. She places a red chord in her window so the Israelites know to save her from the destruction of Jericho.

God said to Joshua, "Have all the soldiers circle the city, marching once around it. Do this for six days, with seven priests carrying ram's horns ahead of the ark. On the seventh day march around the city seven times, and have the priests blow the horns." (Joshua 6:3-4). The soldiers did this and marched silently. Can you imagine what the people inside the city of Jericho must have been thinking of the Israelites? They were probably laughing, but Joshua and the Israelites did as God had commanded, and on the seventh day, God instructed that they march around the city seven times and have the priests blow the horns. They were to shout as loud as they could at the sound of the horns. As they shouted, the walls collapsed, and the Israelites attacked and took the city. Rahab and her household were the only ones saved from the destruction, becoming part of the people of Israel.

Activities:
1. Think about an obstacle (or hard thing) in your life and pray to God to help you overcome that obstacle. Remember God never fails to deliver His promises.
2. Find the ornament with the horn trumpet and hang it on your family Jesse Tree.

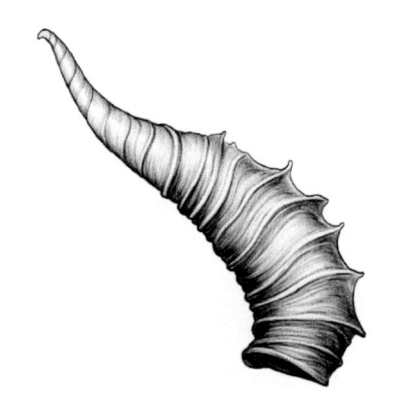

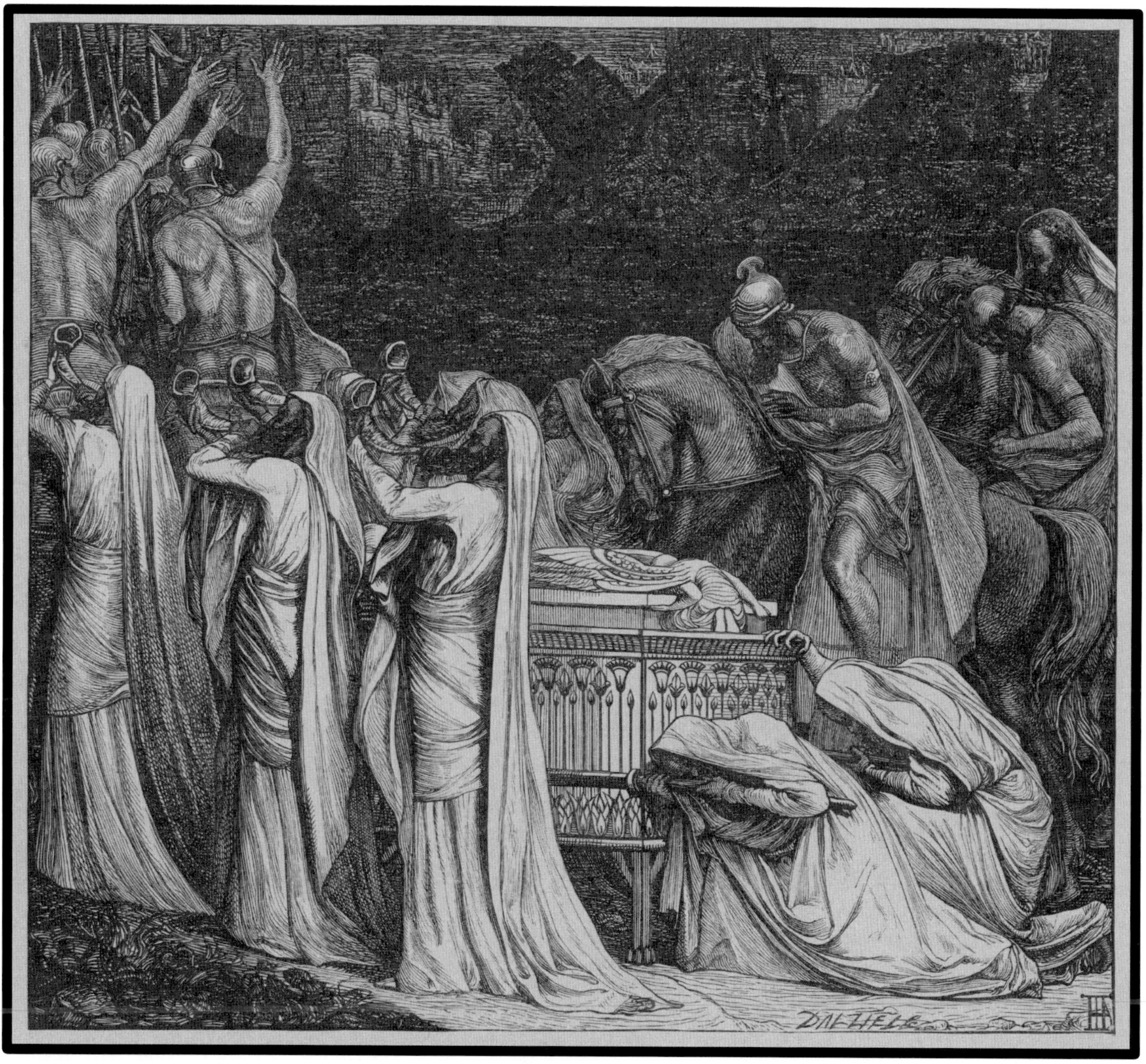
DALZIEL

Day 13

Gideon: A Small Army and an Unlikely Victory
Judges 6-8

The Israelites were blessed for many years, but then they began to disobey God. To help remind them of who He was, God allowed the enemies of the Israelites, called the Midianites, to take their food and animals. The Israelites went hungry. Have you ever felt very hungry? It is not a pleasant feeling.

Starving, the Israelites remembered the Lord and prayed for help. God chose a man named Gideon, a poor farmer, to lead a small Israelite army of soldiers to defeat the Midianites. When the Lord told Gideon that he would be the one leading the Hebrew people against their enemies, Gideon questions God's plan. How could a poor, insignificant farmer defeat the Midianites? God promises Gideon that He will be with him. God commands Gideon to destroy the towns of Israelites worshiping false gods. Gideon did not believe he could defeat the Midianite army, which had more than 135,000 soldiers. Wow! That is a lot of soldiers! Gideon's small army was only made up of 300 soldiers. Who do you think will win the battle?

God gave Gideon wisdom and strength. He instructed his army to use trumpets and lamps to scare the Midianites. The noise and the lights confused the Midianites, who started to fight their own people. The Israelites defeated the huge Midianite army because Gideon had the courage to trust God's plan. God wanted to teach the Israelites that when victory comes, it comes from God, not from themselves.

Activities:
1. At first, Gideon was afraid. Has there ever been a time that you were worried, but God turned your fear into a victory? Take turns sharing with your family.
2. Find the ornament with the soldier and hang it on your family Jesse Tree.

Diruit aram, lucumq̃ Baal, indeq̃ construit aram Domino, et holocaustũ sacrificat.

Day 14

Naomi and Ruth: Ruth's Faithfulness
Ruth 1-4

A woman named Ruth lived in the town of Moab. She was married to one of God's special family members, an Israelite man. Sadly, her husband died. Normally, a woman would return to live with her family if her husband died. Ruth, however, chose to stay with her mother-in-law, Naomi (her husband's mother). Naomi tried to convince Ruth to go back to her own family, saying, "Go back, each of you to your mother's house. May the LORD show you the same kindness as you have shown to the deceased and to me." (Ruth 1:8). Ruth was loyal to Naomi and stayed with her. Ruth told Naomi she wanted the Israelites to be her people and their God to be her God. Ruth did not treat Naomi with kindness to get something in return; she simply wanted to help.

Both of the women went to the town of Bethlehem to try to find work. Back then, men usually cared for their wives, and women did not typically have jobs. So, finding work would be a difficult task. When Ruth and Naomi reached Bethlehem, Ruth began working in a field, picking up leftover barley grain from behind the harvesters (after the grain was harvested, the poor people were permitted to go into the fields to gather any grain left behind). She was a hard worker. The owner of the field, Boaz, was a kind man who believed in God. He noticed how hard Ruth was working and even instructed the harvesters to leave behind extra barley for her.

Boaz and Ruth were eventually married. God blessed them with a baby boy named Obed. Guess what? Jesus is a descendent of Boaz and Ruth. Obed is King David's grandfather and Jesus is a direct descendant of King David. They share a family tree! How neat is it that Jesus shares family lineage with this unlikely couple? God works all things for good for those who love and obey Him. Boaz and Ruth were kind people and faithful servants of the Lord.

Activities:
1. Ruth was faithful and kind to her mother-in-law, Naomi. Boaz was kind to Ruth and took care of her. He was also faithful to God. How do your family members take care of you? How do you show kindness to them? Pick somebody in your family to do something kind for today. Do not tell them you are doing it. Just do it out of the kindness of your heart.
2. Find the grain ornament and hang it on your family Jesse Tree.

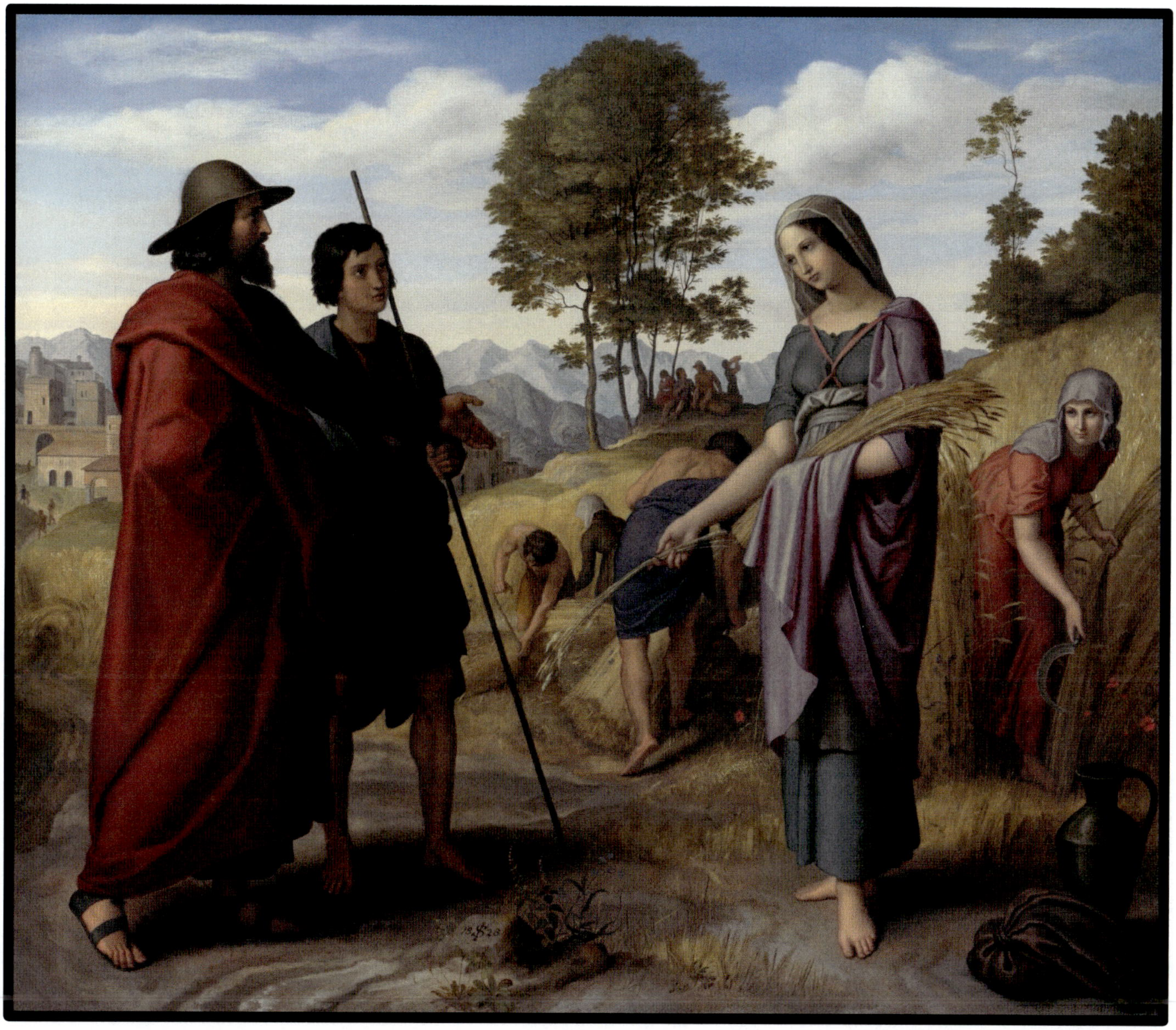

Day 15

Samuel: Beginning of the Kingdom of Israel
1 Samuel 3 & 10-12

Do you know what a prophet is? You will hear that word a lot along the way as you learn about the Bible and Jesus. A prophet is a person who hears from God and then shares God's message with other people. Everything God tells us through a prophet is true. Well, the first time Samuel heard from God, he was just a kid. Samuel lived in a temple with a priest named Eli. Late at night, Samuel heard somebody calling his name. He thought it was Eli calling him. So Samuel responded by going to Eli saying, "Here I am." Eli answered, "I didn't call you; go back to bed!" So, Samuel went back to bed. The second time the Lord called his name, Samuel jumped out of bed and went to Eli saying, "Here I am." Again, Eli said, I didn't call you; go back to bed!" So, Samuel went back to bed. Finally, the Lord called Samuel for a third time. Again, Samuel jumped out of bed and ran to Eli's room saying, "Here I am." This time, Eli realized that it was God who was calling Samuel. Eli told him, "Go and lie down, and if he calls you again, say, 'Speak LORD, for your servant is listening.'" Samuel went back to bed, and sure enough, again, he heard the voice of God calling, "Samuel! Samuel!" Samuel answered as Eli had told him this time, "Speak, for your servant is listening." (1 Samuel 3). Guess what? It was God speaking! He told Samuel He would need to deliver some tough news to Eli. You see, even though Eli was a priest, he had made some wrong choices. God told Samuel that Eli was no longer allowed to be a priest. Samuel was afraid because he thought Eli would be angry about this news. Even though he was scared, he obeyed God and told Eli what God had said. When hearing the news, Eli was upset. He eventually calmed down and said, "He is the Lord; let Him do what He thinks is best." In some situations, people do not like hearing what God has to say if it does not match their plan. Prophets cannot worry about what people say; they must only focus on what the Lord says.

Samuel grew up and became a trusted prophet of the Israelites. Because of this, the Israelites chose Samuel to pick their very first king. God told Samuel that he would send a man from the land of Benjamin to be the King of Israel. That man was named Saul. It turns out that Saul ended up being a lousy king. He made some bad choices. So, God sent Samuel to anoint a new king. He was the smallest and youngest of Samuel's brothers, a humble shepherd boy named David. David grew up to be the greatest king Israel had ever had. You will learn more about David tomorrow!

It is important to remember that God speaks to Samuel even though he was a young child. We must learn to listen for God's voice in our lives. Sometimes, God speaks to us in ways you might not expect: through music, through nature and God's creation, through prayer, through other Christian believers, through the scriptures, through Jesus and the Saints, through your conscience.

Activities:
1. How does God speak to you? Share with your family.
2. Find the lamp ornament and hang it on your Jesse Tree, remembering that His word is a lamp that lights our way. Without Him, we travel in the dark.

SAMUEL declareth to ELI the JUDGEMENTS of GOD upon his HOUSE.

Day 16

David: The Brave and Faithful Shepherd
1 Samuel 16-17

At the time, Saul was the King of Israel, and God was unhappy with him because he had disobeyed God many times. So, God told Samuel, an old prophet, "Fill your horn with oil, and be on your way. I am sending you to Jesse of Bethlehem, for I have chosen my king from among his sons." (1 Samuel 16:1). Samuel was nervous because he thought this would upset Saul, but God told Samuel to bring a young, female cow to sacrifice, and God would tell him what to do. He was going there to anoint the next king that God would choose. So, Samuel did as God asked and made his way to Bethlehem. He invited Jesse and his sons to the sacrifice, and as each son came forward, God told Samuel to reject them as the chosen king. Finally, Samuel saw Jesse's youngest son, David, who was tending to the sheep, and God said, "There-anoint him, for this is he!" (1 Samuel 16:12). So, Samuel took his horn filled with oil and anointed David in front of his brothers, and from that day forward, God would be with David.

At this point, the Spirit of the Lord had left Saul, and an evil spirit was tormenting him. Saul's servants suggested finding someone who could play the harp for him to calm him down, and they suggested David, Jesse's son. They told Saul that David was good at playing the harp, that he was a soldier, and that the Lord is with him. So, Saul told his servants to bring David to him, and Saul asked to keep David in his service because he liked him so much.

In the meantime, the Philistines were preparing for battle against the Israelites, and the Israelites were preparing. A Philistine named Goliath, who was a giant, started shouting at the Israelites to send a man out to fight him. He continued to shout this to the Israelites for 40 days. One day, when David was bringing things to his brothers, who were fighting for the Israelites; David heard Goliath shouting and decided that he should fight Goliath and that he could win. His brothers doubted him. He went to Saul and told him that he could fight Goliath, and again, he was doubted by Saul. Saul said he was only a kid, and Goliath was a giant who had been fighting for years. David defended himself, saying that he tends to the sheep, and when an animal comes to attack his sheep, he kills it. He also said that God will protect him as he was chosen. So, Saul agreed and told David to fight Goliath. David grabbed five stones and his sling and went to fight. Goliath mocked David because he was only a young boy, but David grabbed his sling and stone and struck Goliath in the brow, killing him. David was a hero and went on to be the King of the Israelites for a long time. Even though people doubted David because he was a young boy, he did not give up and had faith in God that he would be protected.

Activities:
1. Has anybody ever doubted you? How did it make you feel? Share your thoughts with your family.
2. Find the ornament with the slingshot and hang it on your family Jesse Tree.

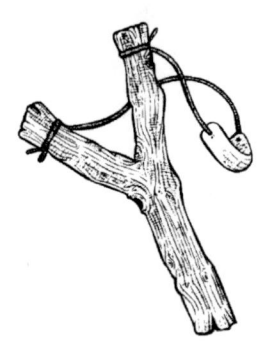

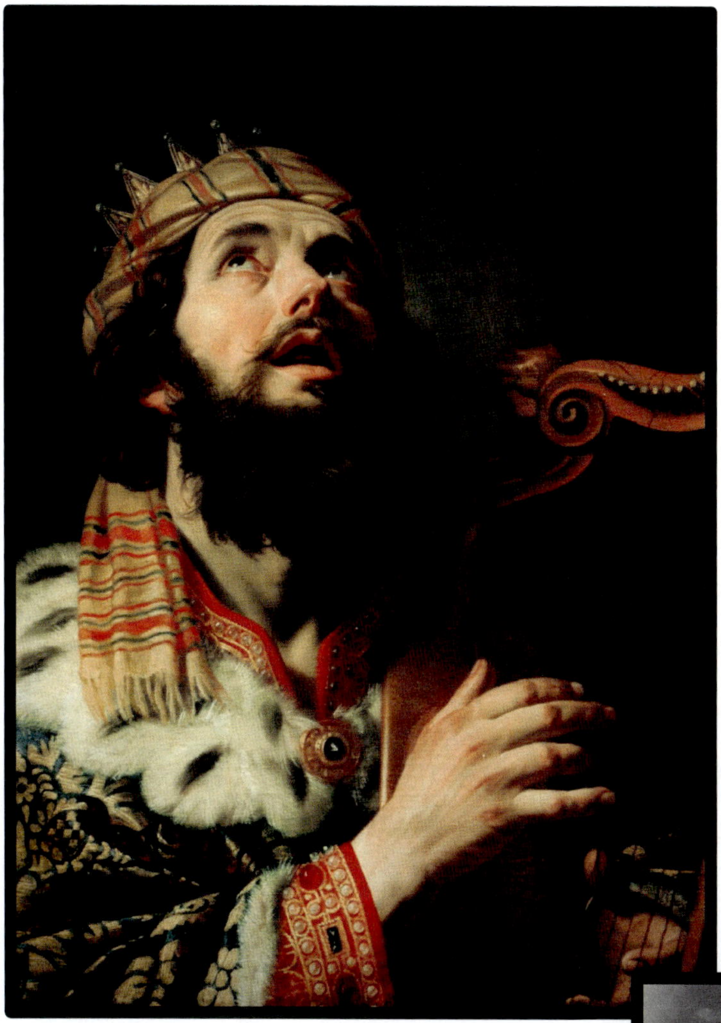

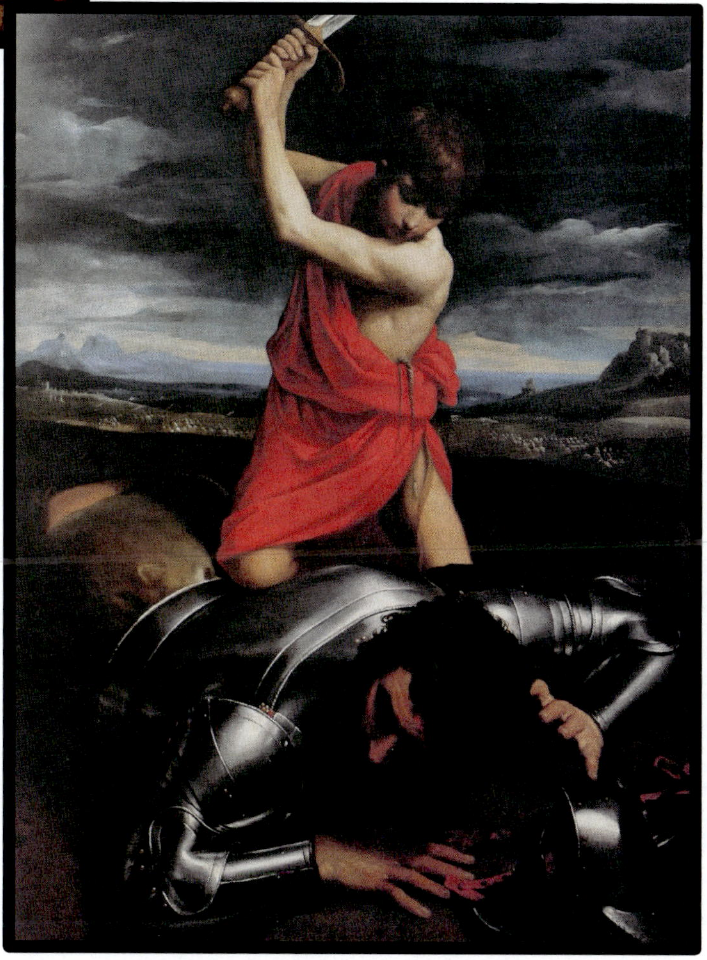

Day 17

Solomon: Prayer for a Listening Heart and the Discernment to Judge Good and Evil
1 Kings 3

Do you remember learning about David yesterday? Well, today, we will learn about Solomon, David's son. After David died, Solomon became the new king. Solomon was a good king and continued to obey God, just as his father did.

One night, while Solomon was in Gibeon, God appeared to Solomon in a dream and said, "'Ask something of me, and I will give it to you." (1 Kings 3:5). Solomon responded by saying, "You have shown great favor to your servant, my father David, because he behaved faithfully toward you, with justice and an upright heart; and you have continued this great favor toward him, even today, seating a son of his on his throne." (1 Kings 3:6). Solomon did not ask God for wealth or riches, but instead he asked for wisdom. He asked God, "Give your servant, therefore, an understanding heart to judge your people and to distinguish right from wrong. For who is able to govern this vast people of yours." (1 Kings 3:9). All Solomon wanted was to be a good leader for his people. So, he asked God to help him know right from wrong, which pleased God.

God was so thrilled that He gave Solomon what he had asked and told him that there would never be anyone as good and as wise as he would be. Even though Solomon did not ask for wealth and riches, God also said He would give him all the riches and a long life, like his father, David, and God did as He said. Solomon lived a long life as a wise king to his people.

Activities:
1. Sit down with your family and think about right and wrong. Talk about things that would make God happy and things that would make God sad. Say a prayer that you can be wise like Solomon and know the difference between good and bad.
2. Find the ornament with the scale and hang it on your family Jesse Tree.

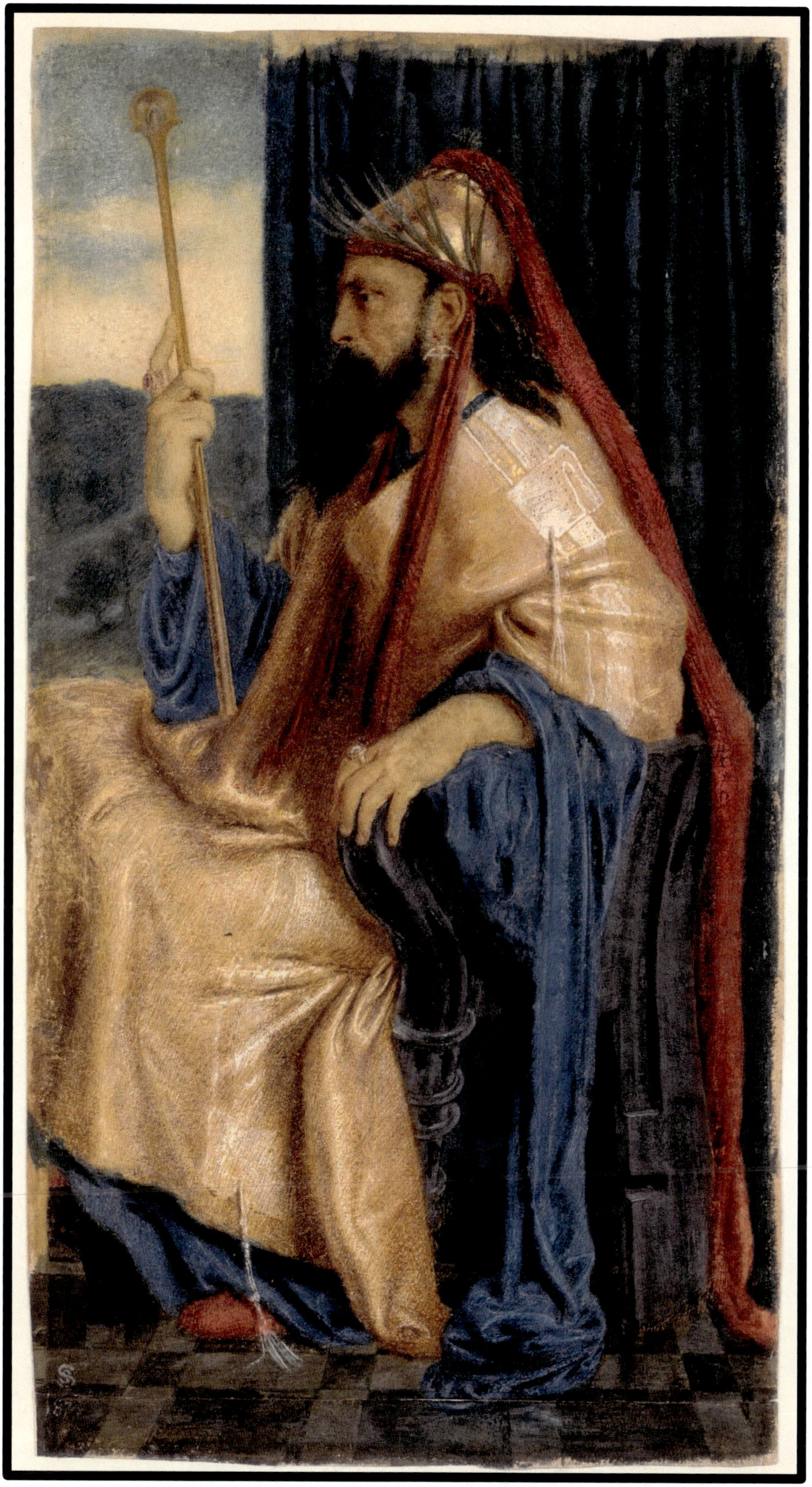

Day 18

Elijah Fights False Gods
1 Kings 17-18, 2 Kings 2

Take a minute to go back and look at Day 11, where we learned about Moses and the Ten Commandments. What is the First Commandment? Today's story will have much to do with the First Commandment, "I, the Lord, am your God. You shall not have other gods besides me." (Exodus 20).

After the death of King Solomon, God's people had many bad kings, but the worst was King Ahab. King Ahab's wife worshiped the false god, Baal, and persuaded Ahab and God's people to worship Baal, too. Because God's people were worshiping a false god, God stopped the rain for a long time. God spoke to Elijah, the prophet, and told him to go to Ahab. Elijah did as God asked and confronted Ahab. He told Ahab that it was wrong to worship a false god, and he told Ahab to have everyone, including the prophets of Baal, meet on Mount Carmel so that he could prove who the real God was.

Once on Mount Carmel, Elijah instructed the people to prepare a bull on the wood but not to start the fire, and Elijah would take the other bull and prepare him on the wood but not start the fire. Whichever bull would catch on fire first would prove who the real God was. So, the people called to their god, Baal, all day, but nothing was happening. Elijah then called the people over and prepared the altar of the Lord. Elijah spoke out to God, and the bull and everything around it set on fire. After seeing this, all the people fell to their knees, admitting, "The Lord is God!" (1 Kings 18:39). Elijah told Ahab to leave before the rain came. God finally sent down rain now that the people no longer believed in a false god.

Activities:
1. Have you ever stood up to somebody who was doing something wrong? Share with your family.
2. Find the ornament with the fire and hang it on your family Jesse Tree.

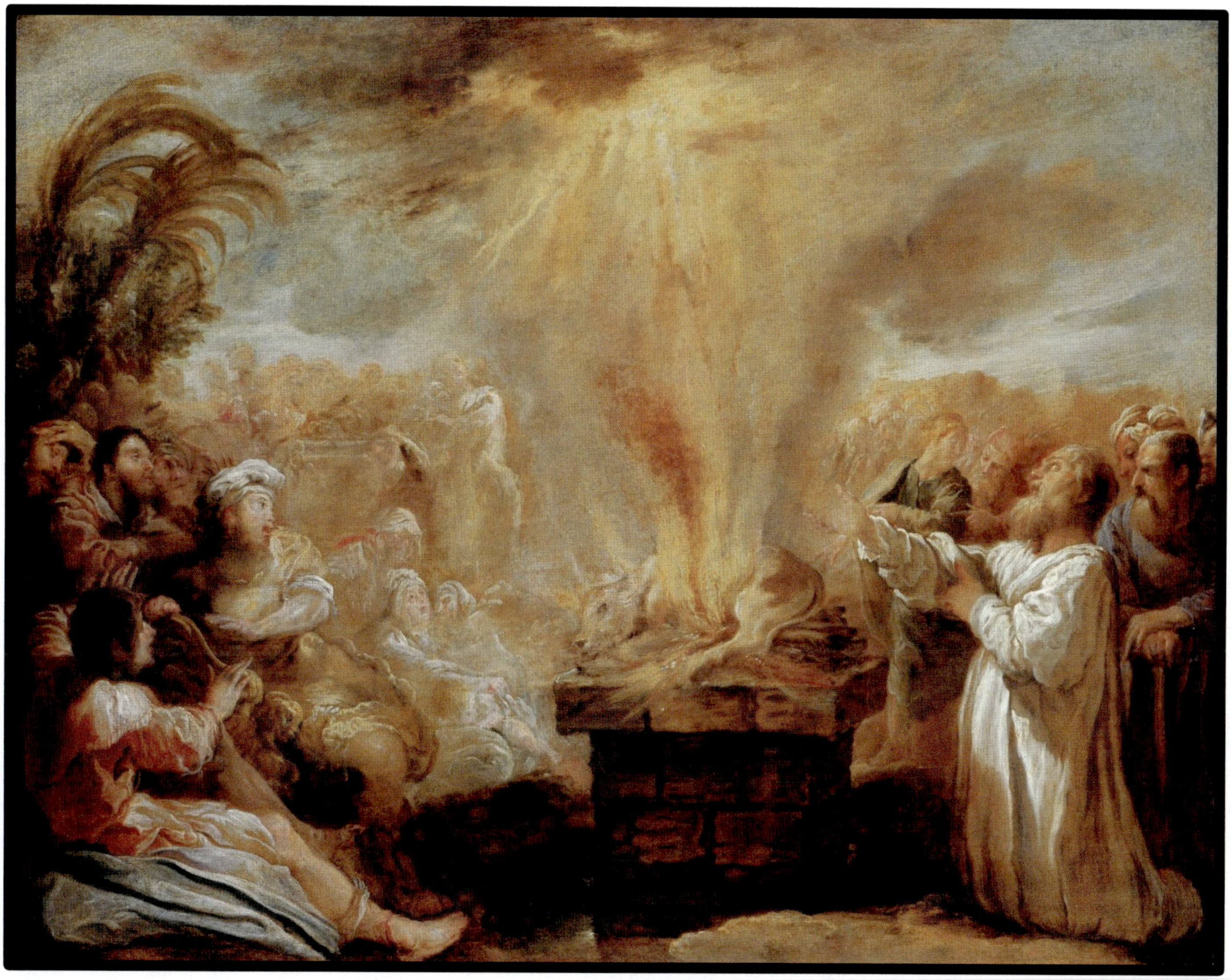

Day 19

Jeremiah the Prophet and His Message of Hope
Jeremiah 7, 26, 28, 29, 31

Yesterday, we learned about Elijah, who was a prophet. Do you remember what a prophet is? In today's story, we learn about Jeremiah, who was also a prophet and messenger, and how he delivered a hard message to the people to turn away from their evil ways.

At this time, God's people were not living according to God's Word. Many of them were worshiping false gods and not treating others with respect. They oppressed widows, orphans, and immigrants. Some also killed others and shed innocent blood. Look at today's symbol (tears) and imagine how sad it would be to live during that time.

At the beginning of the book of Jeremiah, God tells Jeremiah, "Before I formed you in the womb I knew you, before you were born I dedicated you, a prophet to the nations I appointed you." (Jeremiah 1:5). God knew all of us before we were born, and God has a plan for each of us. God continued to tell Jeremiah that He chose him to speak to the people. Jeremiah thought he was too young and could not speak to a crowd of people, but God told Jeremiah that he could and must do it. God let Jeremiah know that He would be with him. Jeremiah went on to say everything God told him to, and he was reminding people that God loved them. Jeremiah even shared stories from the past where God had done marvelous things, but people were angry and did not believe what he was saying. They wanted to kill him, but God protected Jeremiah. Even though the people were doing bad things to Jeremiah, he continued to speak God's message that the people needed to turn back to God.

Activities:
1. Think about a time when you cheered somebody up who was feeling sad. What did you do to help? Share with your family.
2. Find the ornament with teardrops and hang it on your family Jesse Tree.

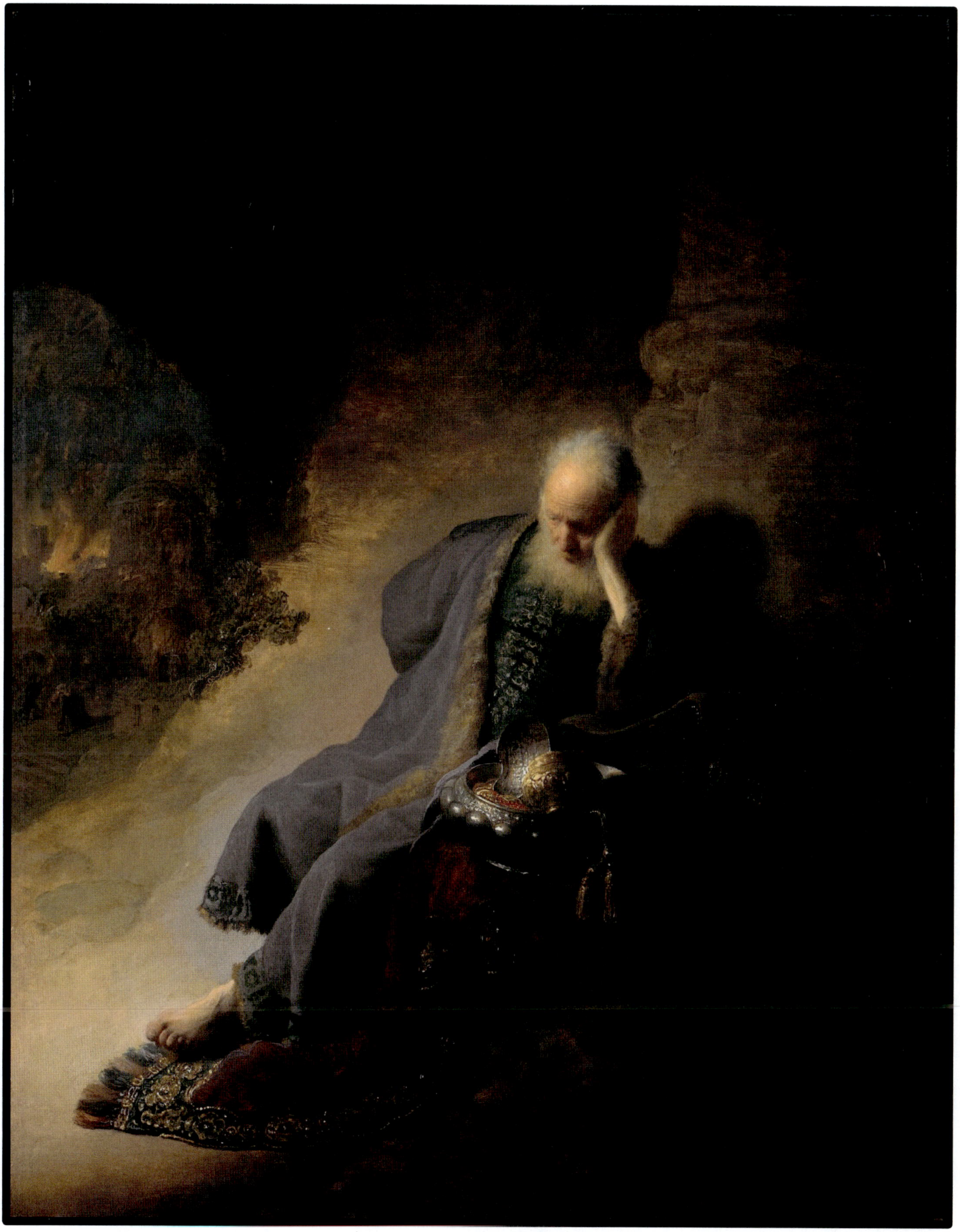

Day 20

Jonah and the Whale
Jonah 1-4

In today's story, we learn about Jonah, a prophet who did not listen to or obey God. Think of a time when you maybe did not listen to God and had to ask for forgiveness. Did it make you feel bad that you did not listen to God?

In Jonah chapters 1-4, God tells Jonah to go to the city of Nineveh and preach to them. God wants them to turn against their wicked ways. Jonah was scared to go to Nineveh, so he disobeyed God and tried to run away by getting on a ship going in the opposite direction. God was disappointed that Jonah did not obey Him, so He sent strong winds to the sea and caused a big storm. All the people on the ship were running around trying to figure out how to save their boat from all the water. Jonah told the people to throw him into the sea since he caused the storm by not obeying God. He thought maybe that would stop the water from flowing into their boat. Although the people were hesitant, they prayed out to God and threw Jonah into the water. They prayed, asking for forgiveness afterward.

God sent a large fish (whale) that swallowed Jonah, and he stayed in the fish for three days and three nights. Jonah sat in the fish, praying to God and asking for forgiveness. God forgave Jonah, and the fish spit Jonah out on the shore. For the second time, God told Jonah to set out to the land of Nineveh to deliver the message He would tell him. This time, Jonah did as God asked, and the people of Nineveh listened and went against their evil ways to believe in God.

Activities:
1. Are you a good listener? Say a prayer to God that He will help you to be a good listener.
2. Find the ornament with the whale and hang it on your family Jesse Tree.

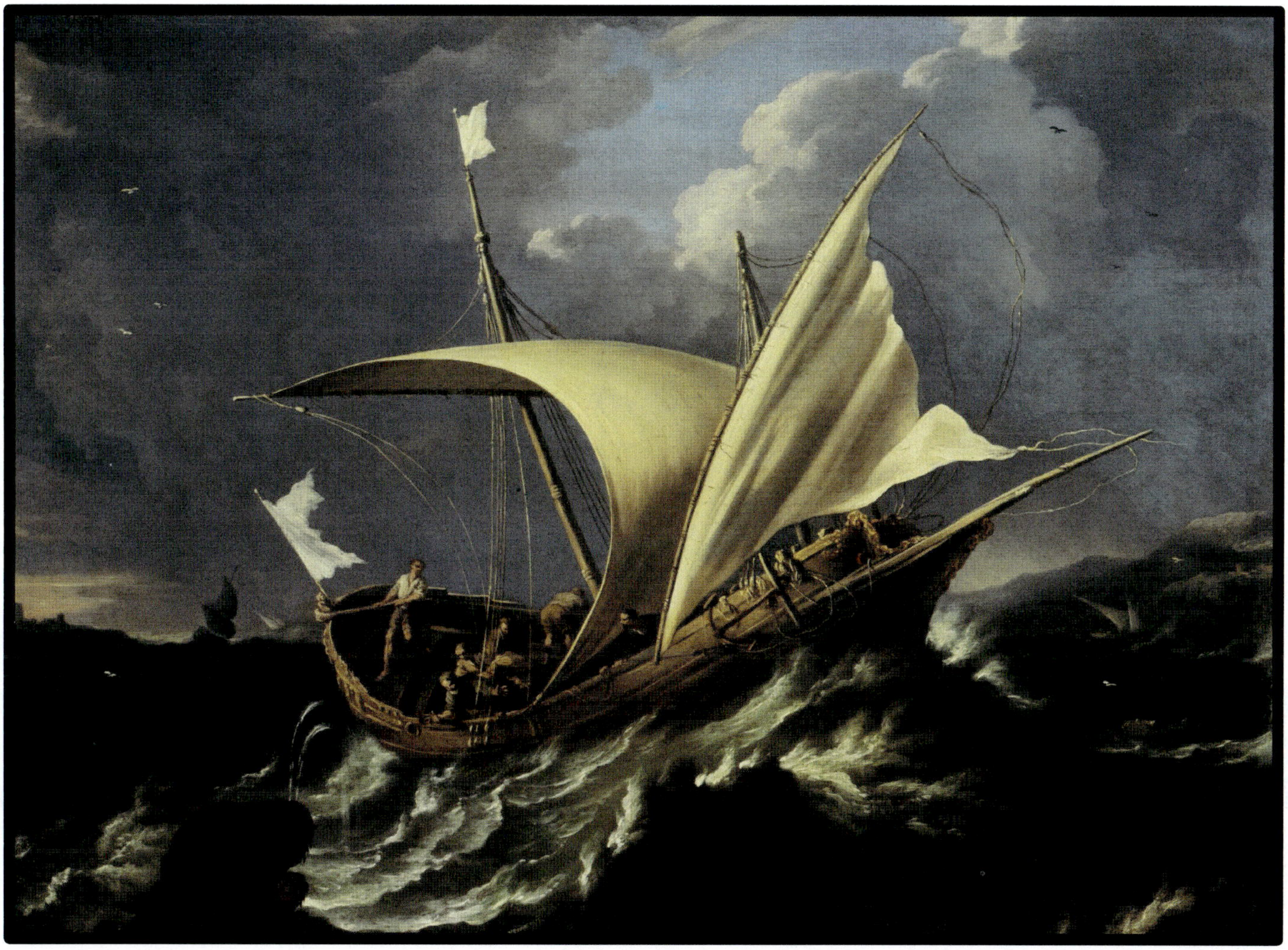

Day 21

John the Baptist: Proclaims the Coming of the Messiah
Luke 3, John 1, Matthew 11

Today, we will learn about John the Baptist, the son of Elizabeth and Zechariah. We will learn more about Elizabeth later, but she is the cousin of Mother Mary. John the Baptist was known for guiding his followers toward Christ instead of calling attention to himself.

John the Baptist was a messenger of God who was preparing the way for Jesus. He spoke to the people about Baptism and repentance and asked the people to change their lives, preparing for the Messiah. Do you know what repentance is? Repentance is turning away from sin and asking for forgiveness. Soon, John started attracting large crowds, and people were coming from far away to hear John preach and to be baptized by him. He would baptize them in the Jordan River and say, "I am baptizing you with water, but one mightier than I is coming. I am not worthy to loosen the thongs of his sandals. He will baptize you with the holy Spirit and fire." (Luke 3:16). Many years later, John would even go on to baptize Jesus in the Jordan River, even though he did not think he was worthy enough to do so. When John baptized Jesus, the Heavens opened and the Holy Spirit came down in the form of a dove. John continued to prepare the way for Jesus to do His ministry on Earth and John followed Jesus the rest of his life.

Activities:
1. Think about your own Baptism. Were you a baby or were you older? Do you have pictures? Talk about it with your family. If you have not been baptized, think about what Baptism means and why it is so important.
2. Find the ornament with the shell and hang it on your family Jesse Tree.

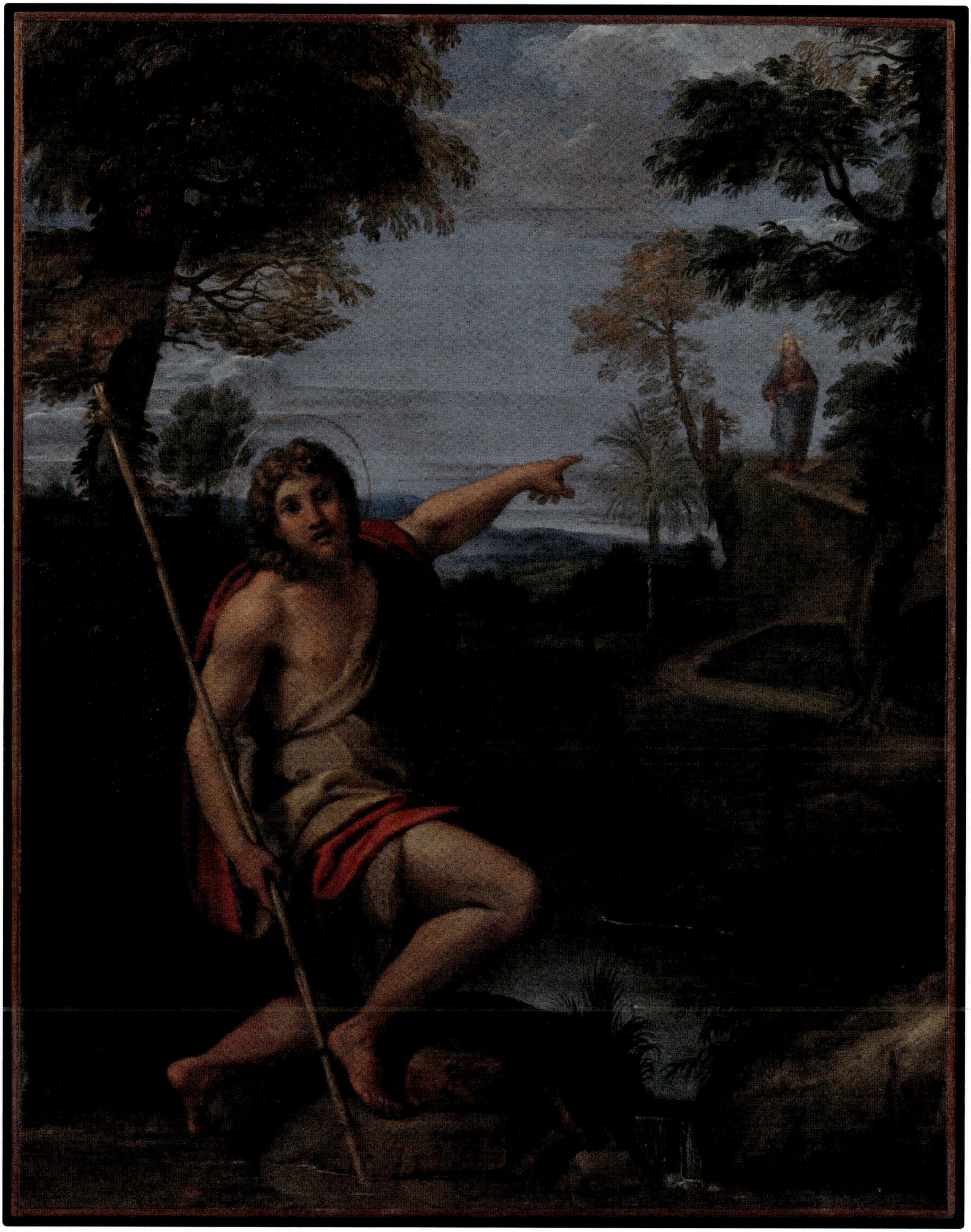

Day 22

Mary: The Mother of Jesus
Matthew 1, Luke 1

Today is a very important day as we will learn all about Jesus' Mother, Mary.

It is important to know that God chose Mary to be Jesus' Mother long before she was born. Because she was chosen to be the Mother of the Son of God, she was born without original sin. Do you remember how we talked about sin when we learned about Adam and Eve? Because of Adam and Eve, we are all born with original sin, which is why we are baptized as babies, to wipe away the sin with which we were born. Well, Mary was born without original sin because she was to be the Mother of Jesus. This is known as the Immaculate Conception, which we celebrate on December 8th.

One day, an angel named Gabriel visited Mary and told her that she would have a baby through the Holy Spirit, and the baby would be named Jesus. "He will be great and will be called Son of the Most High." (Luke 1:32). Mary was confused and scared at first, but the angel told her, "The Holy Spirit will come upon you, and the power of the Most High will overshadow you. Therefore, the child to be born will be called holy, the Son of God." (Luke 1:35). Although Mary was nervous, she decided to trust God and His plans for her.

Mary continued to obey and listen to God throughout her life. When Mary died, she was taken body and soul into Heaven. Mary went straight to Heaven because she did as God asked and led a sinless life, faithful to Him. We celebrate the Assumption of Mary on August 15th. Because of the life Mary lived, she is the Mother of the Catholic church, as well.

Activities:
1. Think about Mary and what you just read about her. On a piece of paper, write a big "M" in the middle of your paper for Mary. All around the "M" write words that describe Mary. Say a prayer to God, thanking Him for Mary.
2. Find the ornament with Mary and hang it on your family Jesse Tree.

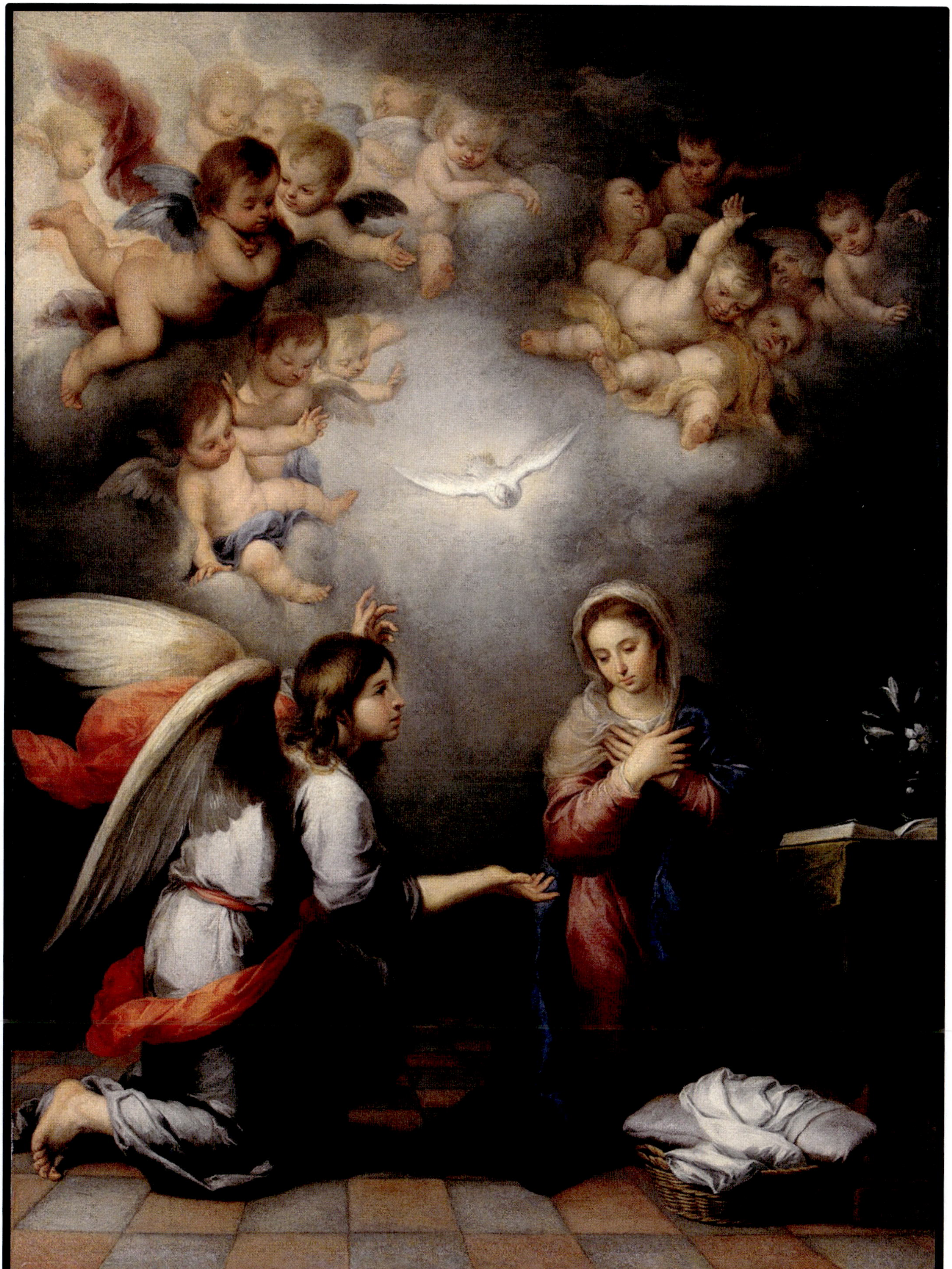

Day 23

Elizabeth: Mary Visits her Cousin Elizabeth, the Mother of John the Baptist
Luke 1

Yesterday, we talked all about Mary, the Mother of Jesus. Today we get to talk about another important woman in Jesus' life, Elizabeth, who was Mary's cousin.

Elizabeth was married to Zecharia, and together they lived according to God's word. Unfortunately, they did not have any children because Elizabeth was barren, which meant she could not have children. Also, Elizabeth and Zecharia were quite a bit older at this time. One day, an angel, Gabriel, appeared to Zecharia and told him that his wife would have a son, and he would be named John. The angel continued that John would go on to do great things and would turn many people to God. Zecharia wondered how this could be possible since he and his wife were so old, but he had faith in God, and Elizabeth did end up being with child.

After the angel, Gabriel, had visited Mary, too, Mary decided to go visit her cousin, Elizabeth. "When Elizabeth heard Mary's greeting, the infant leaped in her womb, and Elizabeth, filled with the Holy Spirit, cried out in a loud voice and said, 'Most blessed are you among women, and blessed is the fruit of your womb.'" (Luke 1:41-42). Does this sound familiar? We hear these words when we pray the Hail Mary. That is so special! Mary stayed with Elizabeth for about three months, and when the time came for Elizabeth to give birth, she gave birth to a son and name him John. This is John the Baptist, who we learned about on day 21, and he grew up to prepare the way.

Activities:
1. Think of the words Elizabeth said to Mary and say the Hail Mary with your family.
2. Find the ornament with Elizabeth and Mary and hang it on your family Jesse Tree.

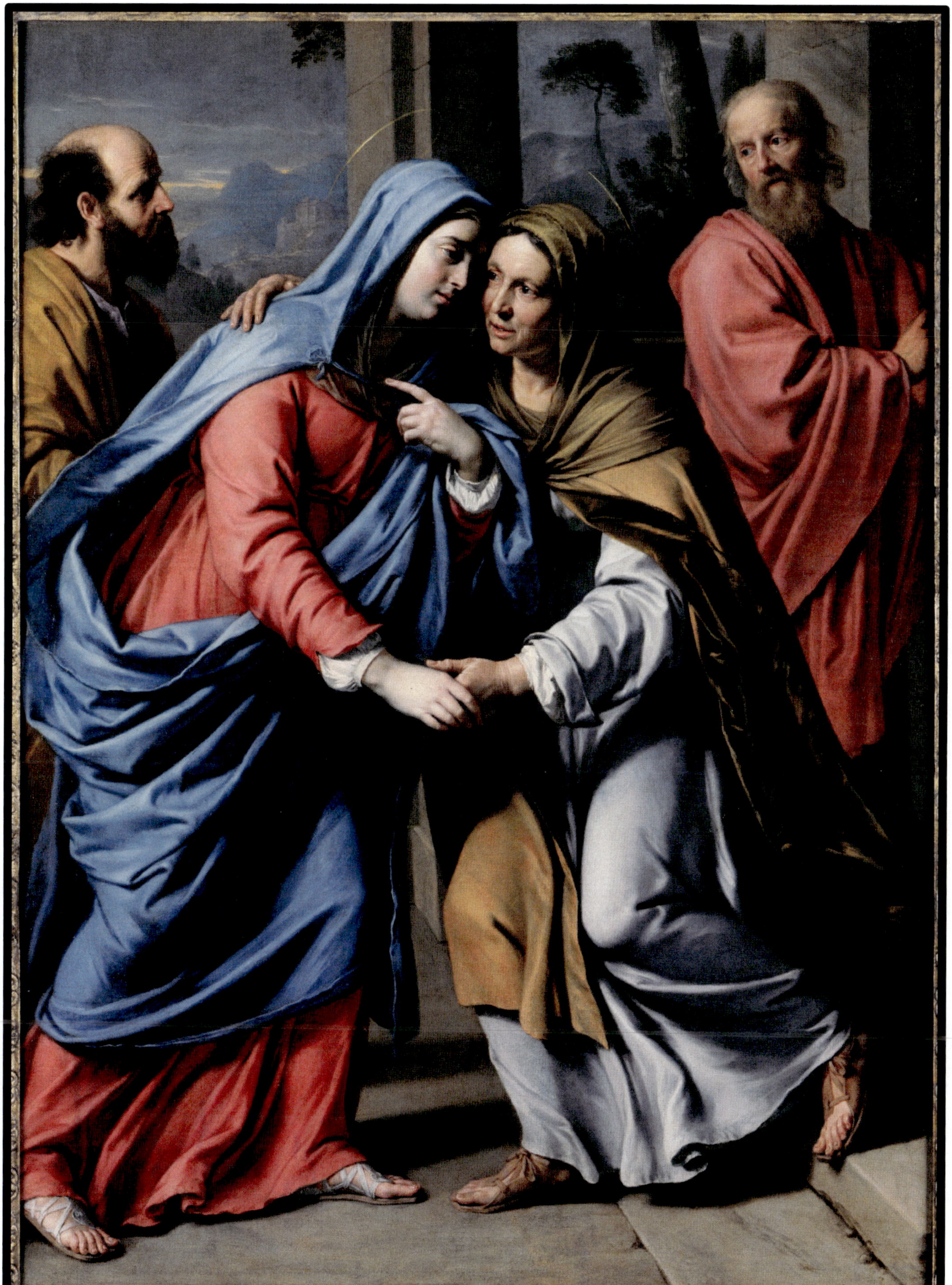

Day 24

Joseph: Mary's Husband and Jesus' Earthly Father
Matthew 1, Luke 2

Joseph was the husband of Mary and the earthly father of Jesus. He was also a carpenter. Do you know what a carpenter is? A carpenter is someone who works and builds things out of wood. Joseph was very good at what he did and was a very good husband to Mary, the Mother of Jesus.

One day, the angel of the Lord appeared to Joseph in a dream and said, "Joseph, son of David, do not be afraid to take Mary your wife into your home. For it is through the Holy Spirit that this child has been conceived in her. She will bear a son and you are to name him Jesus, because he will save his people from their sins." (Matthew 1:20-21). The angel also told Joseph that they should name the child Emmanuel, which means "God is With Us". When Joseph awoke, he did as the angel said and took Mary into his home. He worked hard to protect her and the child she carried.

Together, Joseph and Mary prepared for the coming of Jesus. Although Joseph was nervous and scared at first, he put his faith and trust in God with Mary, and did as God had asked. Throughout the years, Joseph was a wonderful earthly father for Jesus and husband to Mary. Joseph played a significant role in protecting and raising Jesus.

Activities:
1. Look up prayers to St. Joseph with your family.
2. Find the ornament with the toolbox and hang it on your family Jesse Tree.

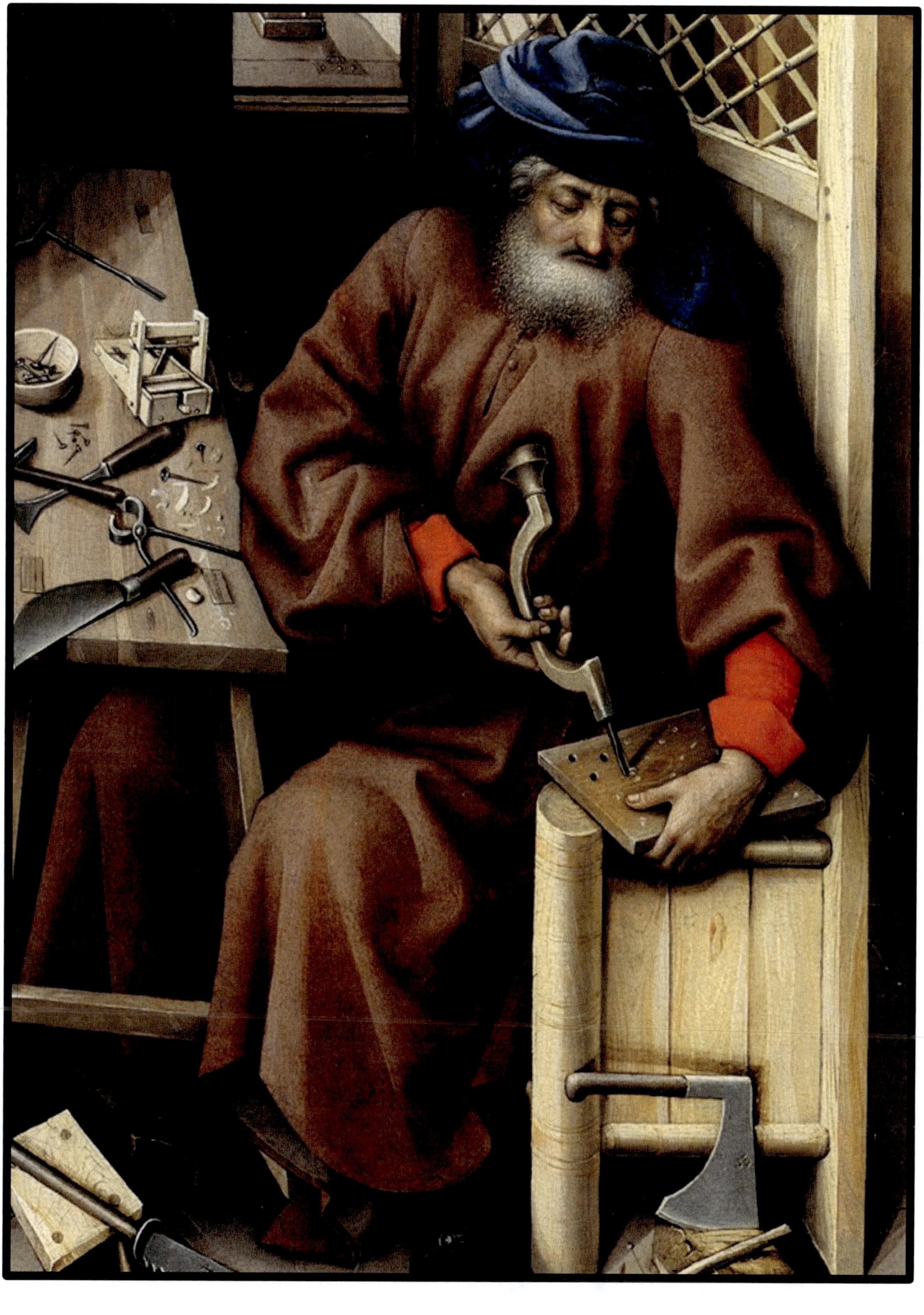

Day 25

Jesus: The Birth of Our Lord
Luke 2, Matthew 2

Merry Christmas! Today, we celebrate the birth of Our Lord, Jesus. A brand new branch has sprouted from the stump of Jesse. This new branch represents Jesus. All our stories have pointed to this joyful day. God gave us the best gift we could ever receive by sending His Son to save us from our sinfulness.

In the Bible, the Gospel of Luke tells us the story of Jesus' birth. Mary and Joseph traveled to the town of Bethlehem. While they were there, Mary gave birth to Jesus in a stable because there was no room at the inn. Can you imagine being born in a small barn? Christ our King is so humble; He came to us as a tiny infant, born in the lowliest of places. Most kings adorn themselves with riches and palaces.

Nearby, in the fields, shepherds were tending their flocks of sheep when an angel appeared, announcing the birth of a Savior. Many angels praised God, saying, "Glory to God in the highest, and on earth peace, goodwill toward men." (Luke 2:14). Have you heard this song at church?

The shepherds hurried to the stable and found Mary, Joseph, and the baby Jesus. After witnessing this, they spread the word about the birth of a King. Meanwhile, in a different Gospel story (Matthew), the wise men, or Magi, saw a bright star that they believed signified the birth of a king. They followed the star to Bethlehem, where they presented gifts of gold, frankincense, and myrrh to the infant Jesus.

Activities:
1. Sing "Happy Birthday" to Jesus!
2. Spend some time with your family looking at the Nativity scene. What do you see?
3. Gaze upon the face of Jesus today, thanking God for sending His only Son to be our Lord, King, and Savior. What a gift!
4. Find the Nativity ornament and hang it on your family Jesse Tree.

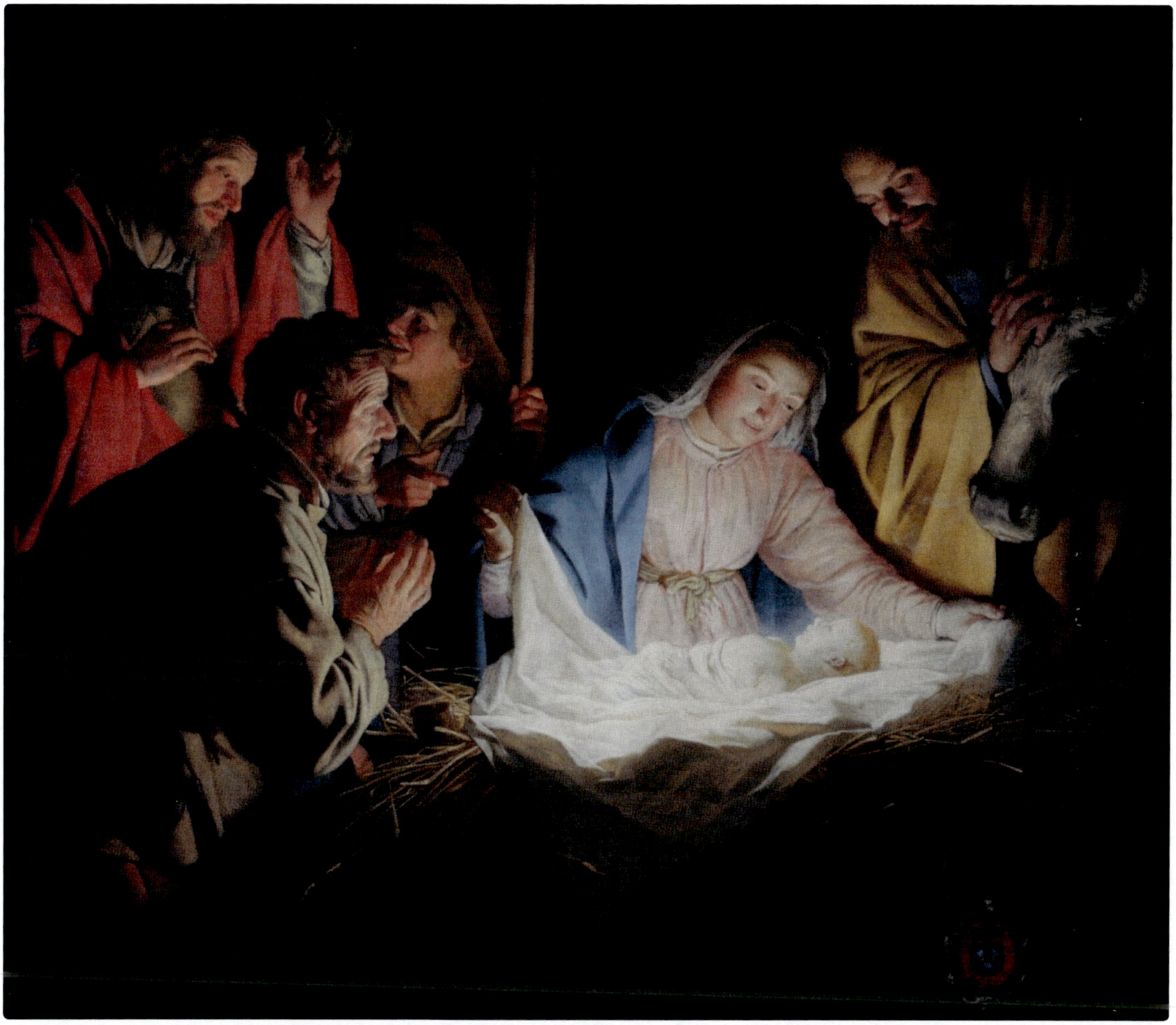

Closing Prayer

Lord God, we adore you because you have come to us in the past. You have spoken to us in the Law of Israel. You have challenged us in the words of the prophets. You have shown us in Jesus what you are really like. Lord God, we adore you because you still come to us now. You come to us through other people and their love and concern for us. You come to us through men and women who need our help. You come to us as we worship you with your people. Lord God, we adore you because you will come to us at the end. You will be with us at the hour of death. You will still reign supreme when all human institutions fail. You will still be God when our history has run its course. We welcome you, the God who comes. Come to us now in the power of Jesus Christ our Lord.

Caryl Micklem, "Contemporary Prayers for Public Worship"

Written and Artistic Sources

Day 1	Stumme, Absolon. Tree of Jesse. 1499. Tempera and gold leaf panel. 214 x 152 cm. National Museum, Warsaw, Poland. https://commons.wikimedia.org/wiki/File:Stumme_Tree_of_Jesse.jpg
Day 2	Van Oosten, Izaak. The Garden of Eden. Between circa 1655 and circa 1661. Oil canvas. 57.7 x 88.2 cm. Toledo Museum of Art, Toledo, Ohio. https://commons.wikimedia.org/wiki/File:Izaak_van_Oosten_-_The_Garden_of_Eden.jpg
Day 3	Peter, Johann Wenzel. Between 1800 and 1829. Oil canvas. 336 x 247 cm. Pinacoteca Vaticana, Vatican City. https://commons.wikimedia.org/wiki/File:Adam_et_%C3%88ve_au_Paradis_Terrestre.jpg.
Day 4	Hicks, Edward. Noah's Ark. 1846. Oil canvas. 772 x 668 in. Philadelphia Museum of Art, Philadelphia, Pennsylvania. https://commons.wikimedia.org/wiki/File:Edward_Hicks,_American_-_Noah%27s_Ark_-_Google_Art_Project.jpg
Day 5	Hult, Adolf. Unknown. 1919. http://commons.wikimedia.org/wiki/File:Bible_primer,_Old_Testament,_for_use_in_the_primary department_of_Sunday_schools_(1919)_(14779694194).jpg
Day 6	Teniers, David. Abrahams Offer. 1653. https://commons.wikimedia.org/wiki/File:David_Teniers_de_Jonge_-_Abrahams_offer_(Kunsthistorisches_Museum).jpg
<u>Day 7</u>	Willmann, Michael. Landscape with The Dream of Jacob. 1691. Oil on canvas. 87 x 106 cm. Staatliche Museen zu Berlin, Germany. https://commons.wikimedia.org/wiki/File:Michael_Lukas_Leopold_Willmann_001.jpg
Day 8	Fiasella, Domenico. Joseph's Coat Brought to Jacob. 1640. Oil on canvas. El Paso Museum of Art, El Paso, Texas. https://commons.wikimedia.org/wiki/File:Giovanni_Andrea_de_Ferrari_-_%27Joseph%27s_Coat_Brought_to_Jacob%27,_oil_on_canvas,_c._1640,_El_Paso_Museum_of_Art.jpg
Day 9	Illustrators Of The 1897 Bible Pictures And What They Teach Us By Charles Foster. The Angel Of Death And The First Passover. 1897. https://commons.wikimedia.org/wiki/File:Foster_Bible_Pictures_0062-1_The_Angel_of_Death_and_the_First_Passover.jpg
Day 10	De Wael, Cornelis. Crossing of The Red Sea. Between circa 1630 and circa 1635. Oil Canvas. 75 x 121.5 cm. Kunsthistorisches Museum, Wien, Austria. https://commons.wikimedia.org/wiki/File:Cornelis_de_Wael_-_Crossing_of_the_Red_Sea.jpg

Day 11	Bol, Ferdinand. Moses Descends from Mount Sinai with The Ten Commandments. 1662. 2840 x 4230 mm. Royal Palace Amsterdam, Amsterdam, Netherlands. https://commons.wikimedia.org/wiki/File:Ferdinand_Bol_-_Moses_descends_from_Mount_Siniai_with_the_Ten_Commandments_-_Google_Art_Project.jpg
Day 12	Camden Press. The Fall of the Walls of Jericho. 1881. Wood engraving on India paper, mounted on thin card. 15.7 x 17.4 cm. Metropolitan Museum of Art, New York, New York. https://commons.wikimedia.org/wiki/File:The_Fall_of_the_Walls_of_Jericho_(Dalziels%27_Bible_Gallery)_MET_DP835823.jpg
Day 13	Van Heemskerck, Maerten. Gideon and His Men Destroying the Altar of Baal. 1561. 20.32 x 24.77 cm. Los Angeles County Museum of Art, Los Angeles, California. https://commons.wikimedia.org/wiki/File:Gideon_and_His_Men_Destroying_the_Altar_of_Baal_LACMA_M.88.91.429b.jpg=
Day 14	Schnorr Von Carolsfeld, Julius. Ruth in Boaz's Field. 1828. Oil Canvas. 59 x 70 cm. National Gallery, London, England. https://commons.wikimedia.org/wiki/File:Julius_Schnorr_von_Carolsfeld-_Ruth_im_Feld_des_Boaz.jpg
Day 15	Daniell, James. Samuel Declareth to Eli the Judgements of God upon his House. 1805. Mezzotint on medium, moderately textured, cream laid paper. Yale Center for British Art, New Haven, Connecticut. https://commons.wikimedia.org/wiki/File:James_Daniell_-_Samuel_Declareth_to_Eli_the_Judgements_of_God_Upon_his_House_-_B1970.3.493_-_Yale_Center_for_British_Art.jpg
Day 16	Van Honthorst, Gerard. King David Playing the Harp. 1622. 65 x 81 cm. Centraal Museum, Utrecht, Netherlands. https://commons.wikimedia.org/wiki/File:Gerard_van_Honthorst_-_King_David_Playing_the_Harp_-_Google_Art_Project.jpg Reni, Guido. David Decapitates Goliath. 1607. Oil on canvas. 174.5 x 133 cm. https://commons.wikimedia.org/wiki/File:David_et_Goliath_guido_Reni_1607.jpg
Day 17	Solomon, Simeon. King Solomon. 1872 or 1874. Egg tempera with touches of technique varnish, paper mounted. 39.5 x 21.5 cm. National Gallery of Art, Washington, D.C. https://commons.wikimedia.org/wiki/File:King_Solomon.jpg
Day 18	Fetti, Domenico. The Sacrifice of Elijah Before the Priests of Baal. Between circa 1621 and circa 1622. https://commons.wikimedia.org/wiki/File:Domenico_Fetti_(Rome_c._1588-Venice_1623)_-_The_Sacrifice_of_Elijah_Before_the_Priests_of_Baal_-_RCIN_405466_-_Royal_Collection.jpg
Day 19	Rembrandt. Rembrandt Jeremiah Lamenting. 1630. Oil on panel. 58 x 46 cm. Rijksmuseum Amsterdam, Netherlands. https://commons.wikimedia.org/wiki/File:Rembrandt_Harmensz._van_Rijn_064.jpg
Day 20	Tavella, Carlo Antonio. Jonah and the Whale. Mid 17th Century. 584 x 838 mm. Royal Museums Greenwich, London, England. https://commons.wikimedia.org/wiki/File:Jonah_and_the_Whale_RMG_BHC0881.tiff
Day 21	Carracci, Annibale. Saint John the Baptist Bearing Witness. 1600. Oil Copper. 54.3 x 43.5 cm. The Metropolitan Museum of Art, New York, New York. https://commons.wikimedia.org/wiki/File:Annibale_Carracci_-_San_Giovanni_Battista_testimone_orsi.jpg

Day 22	Murillo, Bartolome Esteban. The Annunciation. From 1655 until 1660. Oil canvas. 142 x 107.5 cm. https://commons.wikimedia.org/wiki/File:Bartolom%C3%A9_Esteban_Perez_Murillo_023.jpg
Day 23	De Champaigne, Philippe. The Visitation. 1643. Oil on canvas. 114.5 x 88.5 cm. Princeton University Art Museum, Princeton, New Jersey. https://commons.wikimedia.org/wiki/File:De_Champaigne,_Philippe,_The_Visitation,_1643-48.jpg
Day 24	Campin, Robert. Saint Joseph as Carpenter. Between circa 1427 and circa 1432. OIl oak. 64.5 x 27.3 cm. The Cloisters, New York, New York. https://commons.wikimedia.org/wiki/File:Saint_joseph.jpg
Day 25	Van Honthorst, Gerard. The Adoration of the Shepherds. 1622. Oil on canvas. 164 x 190 cm. Wallraf-Richartz-Museum, Cologne, Germany. https://commons.wikimedia.org/wiki/File:Adoration_of_the_shepherds,_by_Gerard_van_Honthorst.jpg
Bible	New American Bible
Front Cover	Van Honthorst, Gerard. The Adoration of the Shepherds. 1622. Oil on canvas. 164 x 190 cm. Wallraf-Richartz-Museum, Cologne, Germany. https://commons.wikimedia.org/wiki/File:Adoration_of_the_shepherds,_by_Gerard_van_Honthorst.jpg
Jesse Tree	Anonymous. (n.d.) The Jesse Tree. www.thebestcatholic.com/bible/tree-of-jesse/
Opening Prayers	Durer, Albrecht. Praying Hands. 1508. Brush, gray and white ink, gray wash, on blue prepared paper. Albertina Museum, Wien, Austria. https://commons.wikimedia.org/wiki/File:Praying_Hands_-_Albrecht_Durer.png
Closing Prayer	Bronzino. Adoration by the Shepherds. 1539. https://commons.wikimedia.org/wiki/File:Worship_of_the_shepherds_by_bronzino.jpg
Symbols	Symbols generated through MIDJOURNEY

Made in the USA
Middletown, DE
11 September 2023